GRADE 4

Reader's and Writer's JOURNAL

SAVVAS
LEARNING COMPANY

ISBN-13: 978-0-328-85159-1
ISBN-10: 0-328-85159-0

22   22

Table of Contents

Name _____

Endings -ed, -ing

Word Bank

watched	watching	danced	dancing	studied
studying	stopped	stopping	dried	drying
happened	happening	noticed	noticing	robbed
robbing	slipped	slipping	hurried	hurrying

DIRECTIONS Use a word from the list that fits each definition. If the verb in the definition ends with *-ed*, write an *-ed* word. If the verb ends with *-ing*, write an *-ing* word.

1. raced _____

2. paying attention _____

3. occurring _____

4. reviewed for a test _____

5. ended _____

6. falling on ice _____

7. moved to music _____

8. observed _____

9. stealing _____

10. dehydrated _____

DIRECTIONS Read the base word at the beginning of each sentence. Write the correct form of the base word to complete the sentence.

11. hurry   Did you see anyone ___by here lately?   11. _____

12. happen   No I didn't. What ___?   12. _____

13. stop   Well, I heard cars ___ quickly.   13. _____

14. dance   People seemed to be ___around in front of the bank.   14. _____

15. rob   Then I realized they were shouting that the bank had been ___.   15. _____

Students apply grade-level phonics and word analysis skills.

Name _____

DIRECTIONS Use each word in a sentence.

squad   assignment   contaminated   population

_____

_____

_____

_____

_____

_____

Write in Response to Reading

DIRECTIONS Reread pp. 6–7 of *Porpoises in Peril*. Write several sentences stating your opinion about whether or not you think it's important for the squad to help the sick porpoises. Support your opinion using details from the text.

_____

_____

_____

_____

Students show contextual understanding of Benchmark Vocabulary. Students write routinely for a range of tasks, purposes, and audiences.

Name _____

DIRECTIONS Research a real person whose achievements have helped others. Then write an introductory paragraph about his or her specific achievements. Your paragraph should clearly establish the topic, introducing the person to your readers and providing details showing why his or her work is important.

_____

_____

_____

_____

_____

_____

Conventions

Nouns Underline one proper noun and circle one common noun in each sentence.

1. Jada and her colleagues gathered in the rain forest.

2. The scientists traveled on two planes in order to reach the Bamboo Inn.

3. Cam organized the plants in his greenhouse carefully.

4. The organization GERA is dedicated to protecting animals all over the world.

5. The eleven-hour flight from Los Angeles exhausted the squad.

Students write routinely for a range of tasks, purposes, and audiences. Students practice various conventions of standard English.

Name _____

DIRECTIONS Use each word in a sentence.

stable   emerged   referring   formulate

_____

_____

_____

_____

_____

_____

Write in Response to Reading

DIRECTIONS Reread pp. 11–13 of *Porpoises in Peril*. Choose a member of the Science Squad, and write several sentences explaining why you think he or she decided to work for GERA. Use details from the text to support your answer.

_____

_____

_____

_____

_____

Students show contextual understanding of Benchmark Vocabulary. Students write routinely for a range of tasks, purposes, and audiences.

Name _____

DIRECTIONS Using evidence from the text, answer the following questions about pp. 11–13 from *Porpoises in Peril*.

1. Reread the two paragraphs on p. 10. How does Jada respond to Cam's question about getting an executive suite?

   _____

   _____

2. What does this tell you about the character?

   _____

   _____

3. On p. 12, why does Reggie begin by referring to Professor Q's report? What does this tell you about him?

   _____

   _____

   _____

4. What key details does the author provide about the porpoises on pp. 12–13?

   _____

   _____

5. What do the characters learn from these key details? How do you know?

   _____

   _____

Students analyze and respond to literary and informational text.

Name _____

DIRECTIONS Write a brief informative paragraph about an animal that lives in the ocean. Your paragraph should clearly establish the topic, introducing the animal to your readers and providing interesting details about it.

_____

_____

_____

_____

_____

_____

Conventions

Form and Use Pronouns Circle the pronouns in the sentences below.

1. Porpoises are animals that live in the ocean. They first appeared millions of years ago.

2. Jada removed her tablet and looked at the information provided by Professor Q.

3. The man clutched his briefcase tightly and ran past the squad.

4. The squad went to speak with Dr. Vloodman because he had reported the problem first.

5. I would love to join the Science Squad after college.

Students write routinely for a range of tasks, purposes, and audiences. Students practice various conventions of standard English.

DIRECTIONS Use each word in a sentence.

rickety   peculiarly   cluttered

_____

_____

_____

_____

DIRECTIONS Reread the fifth and sixth paragraphs on p. 18. Write several sentences explaining what Dr. Vloodman notices about the Science Squad's clothing. Why does he think their appearance will give them luck?

_____

_____

_____

_____

_____

_____

Students show contextual understanding of Benchmark Vocabulary. Students write routinely for a range of tasks, purposes, and audiences.

Lesson 3

Name _____

Nosing Around

Our noses are a treat for our senses. They inhale the delicious smells of baking cookies and sizzling bacon. They also alert us to danger, such as toast burning in a toaster.

Animals also use their noses to smell. However, some animals are capable of using their noses in quite different ways. Have you ever wondered why some animals sport odd-shaped noses?

Elephants have a very familiar odd-shaped nose. An elephant's nose, or trunk, is used for touching, tasting, breathing, and drinking. Did you know that an elephant can use its nose to keep cool in the blazing hot sun? The elephant also uses its nose to reach food that is inaccessible otherwise.

You would think by its name that the elephant nose fish has something special or fascinating about its nose. Indeed, an elephant nose fish is much smaller than a large elephant. However, its "nose" is pretty prominent. Elephant nose fish can be found in muddy waters in Africa. This fish actually uses its long "nose" to seek food in the thick, sticky mud.

The hammerhead shark uses its nose to search for food, too, but in this case, its prey. On the menu for this shark's favorite meal: stingrays. A hammerhead maneuvers its snout to dig stingrays out of their hiding places in the sand. So much for getting buried in the sand to avoid capture!

Then there's the star-nosed mole. This animal has one strange nose! Its nose is covered with 22 tentacles. These tentacles do not have sting cells on them like those of a jellyfish. Still, they help the mole to find food quickly. Insects and worms make favorite main courses for moles. Nosing around could not be more important when it comes to finding these delights.

What all of these animals have in common is an extension that sits somewhere on or near their face. How they use their noses may seem funny to humans, but is the difference between death and survival in the wild.

Students read text closely to determine what the text says.

Name _____

Gather Evidence Circle evidence from the text that shows how the writer organizes the information in this article. Briefly explain how the text is organized.

_____

Gather Evidence: Extend Your Ideas List additional ways informational texts organize information. Then explain how authors organize information in a text to support a reader's understanding of a text.

_____

Ask Questions Underline the names of three animals mentioned in the text. Write three questions you want to research to discover more about one of these animals.

_____

_____

_____

Ask Questions: Extend Your Ideas Write additional questions you could ask about how the animals you identified use their noses differently depending on the habitat in which they live in.

_____

Make Your Case Circle the name of the animal that has the most interesting nose. Underline text evidence that supports your reason for choosing this animal.

Make Your Case: Extend Your Ideas Identify additional reasons that support your opinion. Explain your reasons to a partner.

_____

Students read text closely to determine what the text says.

Name _____

DIRECTIONS Write a one- or two-paragraph biography of a scientist who has made a significant contribution to the world.

_____

_____

_____

_____

_____

_____

_____

_____

_____

Conventions

Relative Pronouns Circle the relative pronouns in the sentences below.

1. There are animals in the ocean that suffer because of human activity.

2. The Science Squad decided to investigate the mining barge, which seemed to disappear mysteriously at night.

3. Dr. Vloodman, whom the scientific community respects, was the first person to report the strange behavior.

4. The man who ran past us was rude and smelly.

5. The report that I got from the researchers wasn't helpful.

Students write routinely for a range of tasks, purposes, and audiences. Students practice various conventions of standard English.

Benchmark Vocabulary

Name _____

DIRECTIONS Use each word in a sentence.

snorkeling   temperature   thermometer

_____

_____

_____

_____

_____

**Write in
Response to
Reading**

DIRECTIONS Reread p. 22 of *Porpoises in Peril*. A snorkeler tells the squad that the porpoises look thin and hungry. What key details does the author provide that might help explain this? Support your answer using text evidence.

_____

_____

_____

_____

Students show contextual understanding of Benchmark Vocabulary. Students write routinely for a range of tasks, purposes, and audiences.

Name _____

DIRECTIONS Using evidence from the text, answer the following questions about pp. 21–24 from *Porpoises in Peril*.

1. Reread the second and third paragraph on p. 21. What does the word *piped* mean?

   _____

   _____

2. What clues did you use to determine the meaning of the word?

   _____

   _____

3. The author tells us that the boy's sister's eyes *widened* when hearing about the porpoises. Why?

   _____

   _____

4. On p. 22, why does the author use the word *alarmed* to describe the snorkeler's mother?

   _____

   _____

5. Reread p. 23. What is a *hypothesis*? How do you know?

   _____

   _____

Students analyze and respond to literary and informational text.

Name _____

DIRECTIONS Write an informative/explanatory paragraph about an animal you have observed frequently or closely. Remember that the purpose of your writing is informative, not narrative. Develop your topic with concrete details that will inform readers about the animal.

_____

_____

_____

_____

_____

Conventions

Simple Verb Tenses Write your own sentences using present, past, and future verb tenses.

1. _____

_____

2. _____

_____

3. _____

_____

4. _____

_____

Students write routinely for a range of tasks, purposes, and audiences. Students practice various conventions of standard English.

Name _____

DIRECTIONS Use each word in a sentence.

    vacant   dredged   depth   scrutinize

_____

_____

_____

_____

_____

_____

_____

**Write in
Response to
Reading**

DIRECTIONS On p. 28 of *Porpoises in Peril*, Jada says to Cam, "Well, that was interesting." What happened that was so interesting? Reread pp. 26–27 and use examples from the text to support your answer.

_____

_____

_____

_____

_____

Students show contextual understanding of Benchmark Vocabulary. Students write routinely for a range of tasks, purposes, and audiences.

Name _____

DIRECTIONS Reread pp. 25–26 of *Porpoises in Peril*. Do some research and then write a paragraph that includes information about porpoises. Your paragraph should include an engaging topic sentence that's supported with facts and details from your research.

_____

_____

_____

_____

_____

_____

Conventions

Relative Adverbs Write your own sentences below using the relative adverbs *where, when,* and *why*.

1. _____

_____

2. _____

_____

3. _____

_____

Students write routinely for a range of tasks, purposes, and audiences. Students practice various conventions of standard English.

Name _____

Base Words, Endings -*er*, -*est*

DIRECTIONS Add –*er* and –*est* to each word on the left. Remember that you may have to double the last consonant, drop the final *e*, or change *y* to *i*.

Word	-*er*	-*est*
heavy	heavier	heaviest
1. great	_____	_____
2. easy	_____	_____
3. thin	_____	_____
4. angry	_____	_____
5. big	_____	_____
6. cold	_____	_____
7. slow	_____	_____
8. long	_____	_____
9. snowy	_____	_____
10. funny	_____	_____

Students apply grade-level phonics and word analysis skills.

Name _____

DIRECTIONS Use each word in a sentence.

conducted   disappointed   recognition   precious

_____

_____

_____

_____

_____

_____

_____

Write in Response to Reading

DIRECTIONS Reread pp. 34–35 of *Porpoises in Peril*. What does the squad learn from looking at Jada's pictures? What connections do they make? Use details from the story to support your answer.

_____

_____

_____

_____

_____

Students show contextual understanding of Benchmark Vocabulary. Students write routinely for a range of tasks, purposes, and audiences.

Name _____

DIRECTIONS Reread the first four chapters of *Porpoises in Peril*. Then retell the events that have taken place so far in your own words. Be sure to include all of the events and to arrange them in the correct order. Use words and phrases that clearly signal a new event in the sequence.

_____

_____

_____

_____

_____

Conventions

Understand Adjectives Circle the adjective in each sentence.

1. The sea horse is an interesting creature.

2. Four squad members climbed the mountain to look for clues.

3. Professor Q wore a striped shirt to the conference.

4. While getting a water sample, Reggie noticed a green fish swimming toward the barge.

5. His cargo shorts were muddied from working in the field.

Students write routinely for a range of tasks, purposes, and audiences. Students practice various conventions of standard English.

Name _____

DIRECTIONS Use each word in a sentence.

focused   enclosed

_____

_____

_____

_____

Write in Response to Reading

DIRECTIONS Reread the second paragraph on p. 43 of *Porpoises in Peril*. How would this paragraph be different if it were written in the first-person? What words would change and why?

_____

_____

_____

_____

_____

Students show contextual understanding of Benchmark Vocabulary. Students write routinely for a range of tasks, purposes, and audiences.

Name _____

DIRECTIONS Using evidence from the text, answer the following questions about pp. 39–43 from *Porpoises in Peril*.

1. Reread the first paragraph on p. 40. What does the author's use of the word *sped* tell you about the squad?

   _____

   _____

2. Reread p. 41. Why do you think the author includes the word *fluid*? Why is this important?

   _____

   _____

3. Reread the first paragraph on p. 42. What does the word *barely* tell you about the opening Kate is going through?

   _____

   _____

4. Why do you think the author includes the word *slowly* in the last paragraph of p. 42? What does this tell you about Kate's situation?

   _____

   _____

5. Reread the second sentence of the last paragraph on p. 43. How does the presence of *cave-like* and *well-lit* help the reader?

   _____

   _____

Students analyze and respond to literary and informational text.

Name _____

DIRECTIONS Research an organization that's dedicated to protecting threatened species around the world. Then write a multiparagraph essay exploring this topic. Be sure to include facts, details, examples, and quotations to develop your topic.

_____

_____

_____

_____

_____

_____

_____

_____

Conventions

Order Adjectives For questions 1–3, underline an adjective in the sentence and then say whether it tells opinion, size, age, shape, color, or origin.

1. The shell I found on the beach is large, round, and blue.

_____

2. An ugly old fish peered at the snorkeler.

_____

3. The elderly American snorkeler wrote a nice letter to the squad.

_____

Students write routinely for a range of tasks, purposes, and audiences. Students practice various conventions of standard English.

Name _____

DIRECTIONS Use each word in a sentence.

evidence   mouthed   dismantle

_____

_____

_____

_____

_____

_____

**Write in
Response to
Reading**

DIRECTIONS Reread pp. 46–47 of *Porpoises in Peril* and look at the visuals on these pages. What do the visuals add to the story? How do the visuals interact with the words on the page? Use examples from the text to support your answer.

_____

_____

_____

_____

Students show contextual understanding of Benchmark Vocabulary. Students write routinely for a range of tasks, purposes, and audiences.

Name _____

DIRECTIONS Create a visual that adds meaning to the informative text that you wrote in Lesson 7. Remember to include a caption to accompany the visual.

Progressive Verb Tenses

1. Change this sentence to present progressive: The boat they rented from the dock was sputtering and swaying.

   _____

   _____

2. Change this sentence to future progressive: The researcher was investigating Dr. Vloodman's complaint.

   _____

   _____

3. Change this sentence to present progressive: They were walking on the beach when the barge's horn blew.

   _____

4. Change this sentence to past progressive: I am swimming quickly toward the shore when the porpoise jumps out of the water.

   _____

Students write routinely for a range of tasks, purposes, and audiences. Students practice various conventions of standard English.

Name _____

DIRECTIONS Use each word in a sentence.

exposed   lurked

_____

_____

_____

_____

DIRECTIONS Reread pp. 8–9 of *Mary Anning: The Girl Who Cracked Open the World*. What do these pages tell you about Mary's life? Use examples from the text to support your answer.

_____

_____

_____

_____

Students show contextual understanding of Benchmark Vocabulary. Students write routinely for a range of tasks, purposes, and audiences.

Name _____

DIRECTIONS Write an informative/explanatory paragraph about Mary's search for fossils. Remember to use vivid language and domain-specific vocabulary.

_____

_____

_____

_____

_____

_____

Conventions

Modal Auxiliary Verbs Read the following sentences, and circle the auxiliary verbs.

1. Mary must get back to the beach as soon as possible.

2. She might be able to find additional fossils near the creek.

3. If you would like, I can look for the fossil before dark.

4. Do you think we should investigate these bones tomorrow?

5. May I use your hammer before the other scientists arrive?

Students write routinely for a range of tasks, purposes, and audiences. Students practice various conventions of standard English.

Name _____

DIRECTIONS Use each word in a sentence.

enormous   encased   magnificent   eagerly

_____

_____

_____

_____

_____

_____

_____

Write in Response to Reading

DIRECTIONS Reread pp. 14–17 of *Mary Anning: The Girl Who Cracked Open the World*. How does the author suggest that Mary is similar to a scientist? Use examples from the text to support your answer.

_____

_____

_____

_____

_____

Students show contextual understanding of Benchmark Vocabulary. Students write routinely for a range of tasks, purposes, and audiences.

Name _____

DIRECTIONS Using evidence from the text, answer the following questions about pp. 10–17 from *Mary Anning: The Girl Who Cracked Open the World*.

1. Reread p. 11. What happened immediately before the events described on this page? What bones does Mary discover?

   _____

   _____

2. Reread the final paragraph on p. 12. What monster is the author referring to?

   _____

   _____

3. In the second paragraph on p. 13, the author says that the bones Mary discovered helped scientists know more about the Earth long ago. Why?

   _____

   _____

4. Reread p. 14. Why isn't Mary mentioned when people talk about the creature that *she* discovered? What does the author tell us on this page that might explain this?

   _____

   _____

5. In the first paragraph on p. 17, the author tells us that Mary borrowed other people's science books. Why didn't she buy her own books?

   _____

   _____

Students analyze and respond to literary and informational text.

Name _____

DIRECTIONS Write a summary paragraph about the events or ideas you plan to write about. Be sure to use correct sentence structure and order your ideas in the appropriate sequence.

_____

_____

_____

_____

_____

_____

Conventions

Sentences Read each sentence below and tell whether the sentence is simple, complex, or compound. Then, underline the word or words that signal a simple, complex, or compound sentence.

1. Mary dug fast. _____

2. We found the bones of an ancient creature, and they're down by the beach. _____

3. Mary wanted to learn everything she could about the world because she cared deeply about science. _____

4. Most scientists didn't realize it, but it was Mary who discovered the ichthyosaur. _____

5. Mary read night and day, as there was so much to learn about the world. _____

Students write routinely for a range of tasks, purposes, and audiences. Students practice various conventions of standard English.

Name _____

Suffixes *-or, -er*

DIRECTIONS Add the suffix to each base word. Then write the new word on the line.

1. edit   +   -or   =   _____

2. conduct   +   -or   =   _____

3. sell   +   -er   =   _____

4. dig   +   -er   =   _____

5. research   +   -er   =   _____

DIRECTIONS Write the word from the box that best fits each definition.

_____   **6.** one who protests

_____   **7.** one who ships packages

_____   **8.** one who directs

_____   **9.** one who dances

_____   **10.** one who bargains

protestor
dancer
shipper
bargainer
director

DIRECTIONS Add the suffix *–er*, or *–or* to each base word in ( ) to make a noun that names the person performing this action. Write the noun on the line.

1. Mary loved to (dig) for fossils.   _____

2. While searching for fossils, Mary would often (gather) bones and rocks into her basket.   _____

3. Some of the students wanted to (protest) the fact that Mary Anning didn't get to name the creature.   _____

4. Mary must wait for the other scientists to (write) her back.   _____

5. The only person to (survive) the lightning strike was Mary Anning.   _____

Students apply grade-level phonics and word analysis skills.

Name _____

DIRECTIONS Use each word in a sentence.

curious   ancient   convinced

_____

_____

_____

_____

_____

Write in Response to Reading

DIRECTIONS Reread pp. 22–23 of *Mary Anning: The Girl Who Cracked Open the World*. How has Mary's life changed since the beginning of the text? Is the scientific community still ignoring her? Use examples from the text to support your answer.

_____

_____

_____

_____

Students show contextual understanding of Benchmark Vocabulary. Students write routinely for a range of tasks, purposes, and audiences.

Name _____

DIRECTIONS Write a paragraph to introduce a scientist whom you admire. You may want to select a scientist who did something notable, such as Benjamin Franklin, who invented bifocals. Begin by consulting a reference book about the scientist you chose. Then select interesting facts and details that explain why he or she is important.

_____

_____

_____

_____

_____

_____

Conventions

Complete Sentences Read the following sentence fragments. Rewrite them to make complete sentences.

1. Mary Anning was interested in.

_____

2. Because she studied every day.

_____

3. Yesterday when I discovered.

_____

4. Mary's close friend.

_____

Students write routinely for a range of tasks, purposes, and audiences. Students practice various conventions of standard English.

Name _____

DIRECTIONS Use each word in a sentence.

plaster   accomplish

_____

_____

_____

_____

**Write in
Response to
Reading**

DIRECTIONS Reread the final paragraph on p. 27 of *Mary Anning: The Girl Who Cracked Open the World*. Who is Louis and why is he grateful? Why does he name two fossils after Mary? Use specific examples from pp. 25–27 to support your answer.

_____

_____

_____

_____

_____

Students show contextual understanding of Benchmark Vocabulary. Students write routinely for a range of tasks, purposes, and audiences.

Name _____

DIRECTIONS Using evidence from the text, answer the following questions about pp. 25–32 from *Mary Anning: The Girl Who Cracked Open the World*.

1. Reread the first paragraph on p. 25. What is the main idea?

   _____

   _____

2. What details does the author provide to support the main idea?

   _____

   _____

3. Reread pp. 26–27. What details from the text could you use to support the idea that Mary is influential?

   _____

   _____

4. Reread 29–30. What details from the text could you use to support the idea that Henry was Mary's close friend?

   _____

   _____

5. In the final paragraph on p. 31, the author tells us that Mary "helped change the world of science." Do you agree with the author? Choose two details from pp. 25–32 to support your answer.

   _____

   _____

Students analyze and respond to literary and informational text.

Name _____

DIRECTIONS Plan and prewrite an informative/explanatory piece about one aspect of Mary Anning's work. Revisit the text to identify a topic for research. Then write a guiding question to guide your research.

_____

_____

_____

_____

_____

Prepositional Phrases Circle the prepositional phrase(s) in the sentences below.

1. At the Geological Society, Dr. Henry spoke fondly of his dear friend Mary Anning.

2. The scientists lugged their digging equipment down the beach.

3. We wandered through the museum and thought about Mary Anning's discoveries.

4. I enjoy thinking about how many fossils must be hidden under the sea.

5. Is it strange that Mary located so many fossils at the beach?

Students write routinely for a range of tasks, purposes, and audiences. Students practice various conventions of standard English.

Name _____

DIRECTIONS Use each word in a sentence.

emerged   skeleton   curious   accomplish

_____

_____

_____

_____

_____

_____

_____

**Write in
Response to
Reading**

DIRECTIONS Reread *Porpoises in Peril* and *Mary Anning: The Girl Who Cracked Open the World*. What do the members of the Science Squad and Mary Anning have in common? Do you think they would get along if they met each other? Use specific examples from the text to support your answer.

_____

_____

_____

_____

_____

Students show contextual understanding of
Benchmark Vocabulary. Students write routinely
for a range of tasks, purposes, and audiences.

A "Coat" of Many Colors

Life can be tough for some animals. Imagine spending most of your life either looking for food or trying to avoid becoming food for predators. Yet one or both of these tasks are necessary for individuals and species to survive.

How does a lion sneak up on its prey without being seen? How can an insect protect itself from birds looking for a tasty snack? How do little fish avoid becoming prey to bigger fish? Whether you are a predator or prey, the ability to seem to disappear into your surroundings is a huge advantage.

The word camouflage comes from a French word meaning "to disguise." A camouflaged animal takes on the appearance of its surroundings. Lions seem to disappear into the tall grass of the savanna. This allows them to sneak up on their prey without being seen. Squirrel fur is rough, uneven, and a grey-brown color. To a hawk or eagle looking for food, the squirrel looks like tree bark. Some insects have a hard shell that looks like dead leaves or branches.

Reptiles, amphibians, and fish are covered in scales. They produce colored pigments called biochromes. These pigments may be in skin cells or at deeper levels of the body. As some animals move from one background to another, they can quickly change color to match, making them nearly invisible. Also, some sea creatures, such as certain species of nudibranch (NOO duh brangk), change color by changing their diet. Their bodies take on the color of the coral they eat, so they become almost invisible. Imagine what it would be like to possess an ability like that!

What about birds, whose coloring is in their feathers? Birds can't change color quickly, but many birds do change color with the seasons. Varying temperatures or hours of daylight cause these birds to grow a new set of feathers as the background changes. For example, a bird that is mainly brown in summer may change to white in winter.

Camouflage abilities develop gradually through the process of natural selection. For example, if an individual animal's coloring closely matches its surroundings, predators are less likely to devour it. As a result, it survives to produce offspring. These offspring inherit the same coloration, so they also live long enough to pass it on.

Students read text closely to determine what the text says.

Name _____

Gather Evidence Circle the names of animals that change color and underline what causes their color to change. Write the name of each animal and what causes it to change color below.

_____

_____

Gather Evidence: Extend Your Ideas Briefly explain how color change is important to each animal's survival.

_____

_____

Ask Questions Draw a box around the name of one animal you would like to know more about. Write two questions about how this animal uses camouflage that you would like to ask an expert.

_____

_____

Ask Questions: Extend Your Ideas Write additional questions you have about how animals use camouflage to find food or to avoid becoming food.

_____

_____

Make Your Case Look back at the circled animal names and underlined causes for their color changes. Identify how the writer organized, or ordered, the information. Write this method of organization in the margin on the page.

_____

_____

Make Your Case: Extend Your Ideas Would you organize the information the same way? Explain why or why not. Include at least two reasons.

_____

_____

Students read text closely to determine what the text says.

Name _____

DIRECTIONS Begin drafting the one-page informative paper you began in Lessons 11 and 12. Focus on getting your ideas on paper, using concrete words and phrases, and grouping related information.

_____

_____

_____

_____

_____

_____

Conventions

Writing Complete Sentences Change the following run-on sentences to complete sentences by punctuating them correctly.

1. Mary's friend always supported her he never let her down.

_____

2. The fossils kept piling up she had to find a new basket.

_____

3. Jada searched the seabed for evidence of porpoise activity she didn't find any.

_____

4. The scientific community didn't believe Mary there was little reason for this.

_____

Students write routinely for a range of tasks, purposes, and audiences. Students practice various conventions of standard English.

Name _____

DIRECTIONS Use each word in a sentence.

international   surveyed   extinction   juvenile

_____

_____

_____

_____

_____

_____

_____

Write in Response to Reading

DIRECTIONS Reread p. 6 of "Fragile Frogs." What main idea is the writer exploring on this page? What details does the writer give to support this main idea? Write an expository paragraph to describe the main idea and key details. Support your ideas using text evidence.

_____

_____

_____

_____

_____

Students show contextual understanding of Benchmark Vocabulary. Students write routinely for a range of tasks, purposes, and audiences.

Name _____

DIRECTIONS Using evidence from the text, answer the following questions about pp. 5–8 from "Fragile Frogs."

1. Reread the first paragraph on p. 5. What main idea is the writer trying to explore?

   _____

   _____

2. What is one detail that supports this main idea?

   _____

   _____

3. What is one idea that supports the main idea that the gastric brooding frog was a remarkable species?

   _____

   _____

4. Reread the second paragraph on p. 6. What main idea is the writer exploring in this paragraph?

   _____

   _____

5. What do you think the author wants us to think about by writing about fragile frogs?

   _____

   _____

Students analyze and respond to literary and informational text.

Name _____

DIRECTIONS Continue with your draft of the paper you worked on in Lessons 11–13. Focus on organizing your ideas and information in a way that makes sense. Remember to check your introduction, body paragraphs, and conclusion.

_____

_____

_____

_____

_____

_____

_____

_____

_____

Conventions

Modal Auxiliaries Underline the auxiliary verb in the following sentences.

1. Yet hidden deformities can still harm frogs.

2. The frog scientist must help the species before it goes extinct.

3. Pollution in the atmosphere can affect the development of frogs.

4. The students may go into the jungle tomorrow morning to study the frogs.

5. Citizens around the world must understand the problems that many animal species are facing.

 Students write routinely for a range of tasks, purposes, and audiences. Students practice various conventions of standard English.

Name _____

DIRECTIONS Use each word in a sentence.

altitudes   native   exposed   vulnerable

_____

_____

_____

_____

_____

_____

_____

Write in Response to Reading

DIRECTIONS Reread p. 9 of "Fragile Frogs." In the final paragraph, the author says that frogs face "not just one threat but many." Select one of the species mentioned on p. 9, and explain the specific threats that it's facing. Use specific examples from the text to support your answer.

_____

_____

_____

_____

Students show contextual understanding of Benchmark Vocabulary. Students write routinely for a range of tasks, purposes, and audiences.

Name _____

DIRECTIONS Reread your draft. Add linking words and phrases wherever possible to strengthen the flow of your writing and improve the relationship between your ideas. Use the models in the text as a guide.

_____

_____

_____

_____

_____

_____

_____

Conventions

Use Correct Capitalization Correctly capitalize the proper nouns in the following sentences.

1. new Zealand has many different species of frogs.

_____

2. california's red-legged frog has been hit by a truckload of problems: habitat loss, fungal disease, and introduced bullfrogs.

_____

_____

3. Blue poison dart frogs live in south america.

Students write routinely for a range of tasks, purposes, and audiences. Students practice various conventions of standard English.

Compound Words

Word Bank

watermelon	homemade	sometimes	shoelace	highway
shortcut	doorbell	jellyfish	campfire	anyway
fireworks	haircut	loudspeaker	laptop	flashlight

DIRECTIONS Write the correct list word beside its definition.

1. portable light powered by batteries   1. _____

2. hairstyle; trim   2. _____

3. display of exploding chemicals   3. _____

4. more direct route; easier way of performing task   4. _____

5. occasionally; not in every case   5. _____

6. main road   6. _____

7. device to signal that a visitor has arrived   7. _____

8. clear, transparent marine animal with tentacles   8. _____

9. outdoor stack of burning wood   9. _____

10. nevertheless; no matter what   10. _____

DIRECTIONS Use a word from the word list to complete each sentence.

11. A cold, juicy slice of _____ tastes great on a hot summer day.   11. _____

12. Tie that _____ so you don't trip.   12. _____

13. Mom bakes the most delicious _____ apple pies.   13. _____

14. Did you hear the announcement that just came over the _____?   14. _____

15. My _____ computer has a very small screen.   15. _____

Students apply grade-level phonics and word analysis skills.

Name _____

DIRECTIONS Use each word in a sentence.

extinction   vulnerable

_____

_____

_____

_____

Write in Response to Reading

DIRECTIONS Examine the revisited reading from *Porpoises in Peril*. Identify an important point the author is making. Write an opinion paragraph in which you identify the reasons and evidence the author uses to support this point. Then explain whether you find this support convincing.

_____

_____

_____

_____

_____

Students show contextual understanding of Benchmark Vocabulary. Students write routinely for a range of tasks, purposes, and audiences.

Name _____

DIRECTIONS Answer the questions below using evidence from *Porpoises in Peril*, *Mary Anning: The Girl Who Cracked Open the World*, and "Fragile Frogs."

1. Reread pp. 36–39 of *Porpoises in Peril*. What evidence does the Science Squad have so far that suggests Drake Darkly is responsible for harming the porpoises?

   _____

   _____

2. Reread the second paragraph on p. 14 of *Mary Anning: The Girl Who Cracked Open the World*. What is the main idea of this paragraph?

   _____

   _____

3. What is one piece of evidence the author uses to support this idea?

   _____

   _____

4. Reread the final paragraph on p. 9 of "Fragile Frogs." What is the main point the writer is trying to make in this paragraph?

   _____

   _____

5. What evidence does the writer use to support this point?

   _____

   _____

Students analyze and respond to literary and informational text.

Name _____

DIRECTIONS Craft a strong conclusion to the informative piece that you began in Lesson 11. Think about your main topic and most important points. Be sure to restate these main points clearly and concisely. Your conclusion should include a clincher to make it more engaging and interesting.

_____

_____

_____

_____

Conventions

Punctuate Direct Speech and Quotations Correctly punctuate each of the sentences below.

1. Reggie turned to Jada and said, I can't believe we managed to stop Drake Darkly.

_____

_____

2. "I noticed something unusual in the mine, she said, and it really concerns me."

_____

_____

3. The fossil was so large that it took several people to move," said Henry.

_____

_____

Students write routinely for a range of tasks, purposes, and audiences. Students practice various conventions of standard English.

Name _____

DIRECTIONS Use each word in a sentence.

assignment   evidence   curious   surveyed

_____

_____

_____

_____

_____

Write in Response to Reading

DIRECTIONS Write a summary of each of the three texts. Be sure to include the main idea of each text and the key details that support it.

_____

_____

_____

_____

_____

_____

Students show contextual understanding of Benchmark Vocabulary. Students write routinely for a range of tasks, purposes, and audiences.

Name _____

DIRECTIONS Revise, edit, and proofread your informative paper on Mary Anning's work. Check to be sure that you have included all relevant information and deleted any irrelevant or repeated information. Pay close attention to the spelling of proper nouns like the names of people and places.

_____

_____

_____

_____

_____

_____

Conventions

Punctuate Dialogue For questions 1–3, circle the quotation marks and punctuation marks inside the quote. Then write your own sentences using dialogue.

1. "No, you're not running away from the Science Squad!"

2. Mary looked directly at the fossil and said to herself, "This is huge!"

3. "Sometimes the chemicals people use have unintended consequences for animals," said Tyrone, "so it's best to learn as much as we can."

4. _____

   _____

5. _____

   _____

Students write routinely for a range of tasks, purposes, and audiences. Students practice various conventions of standard English.

Name _____

DIRECTIONS Use each word in a sentence.

temperature   international   exposed

_____

_____

_____

_____

_____

**Write in
Response to
Reading**

DIRECTIONS Compare the purposes and effects of each of the three texts. Include examples from the texts to support your ideas.

_____

_____

_____

_____

_____

_____

Students show contextual understanding of Benchmark Vocabulary. Students write routinely for a range of tasks, purposes, and audiences.

Name _____

DIRECTIONS Format and publish the revised, edited version of your informative writing piece. Draft a plan for your presentation, alter your writing as necessary, and practice presenting your topic. You should be ready to present your work to the class.

Conventions

Frequently Confused Words Add the words *to, two, too, there,* or *their* to the sentences below.

1. Reggie transported _____ opals back _____ Hiram College.

2. Mary wanted recognition for her work, _____.

3. The researchers had _____ venture deep into the jungle to retrieve _____ equipment.

4. _____ is no way to know for sure which chemical is causing this disease.

5. "Would you like one or _____ water samples?" Jada asked. "_____ is plenty of time to collect them."

Students write routinely for a range of tasks, purposes, and audiences. Students practice various conventions of standard English.

Suffixes *-ist, -ive, -ness*

DIRECTIONS Add the suffix to each base word and write the new word on the line.

1. adapt   +   -ive   =   _____

2. art   +   -ist   =   _____

3. great   +   -ness   =   _____

4. biology +   -ist   =   _____

5. fair   +   -ness   =   _____

DIRECTIONS Write the word from the box that best fits each definition.

_____   6. a doctor who cares for your teeth

_____   7. a person who drives motorcars

_____   8. a person who sells flowers

_____   9. a scientist in the field of chemistry

_____   10. a person who makes art

| chemist |
| dentist |
| motorist |
| artist |
| florist |

DIRECTIONS Add the suffix *-ist, -ive,* or *-ness* to the base word in ( ) to complete each sentence. Use the words in the box to help. Write the word on the line.

_____   11. Her argument was quite (persuade).

_____   12. The (firm) of his mattress was unpleasant.

_____   13. The battery was (defect).

_____   14. Instead, she traveled as a (tour).

_____   15. The (calm) with which he addressed the unruly crowd was unexpected.

| calmness |
| defective |
| firmness |
| persuasive |
| tourist |

Students apply grade-level phonics and word analysis skills.

Lesson 1

Name _____

DIRECTIONS Use each word below in a sentence.

supports   framework   expand

_____

_____

_____

_____

_____

Write in Response to Reading

DIRECTIONS Reread p. 5 of *Skeletons Inside and Out*. Write several sentences explaining how an exoskeleton is different from an endoskeleton. Use text evidence to support your answer.

_____

_____

_____

_____

_____

Students show contextual understanding of Benchmark Vocabulary. Students write routinely for a range of tasks, purposes, and audiences.

Name _____

DIRECTIONS Choose an animal, and write a brief introductory paragraph about the animal. Paragraphs should clearly establish the topic, introducing the animal to readers and providing details about its traits, or features. Be sure that the topic is clearly explained and easily understandable for readers.

_____

_____

_____

_____

_____

_____

Conventions

Form and Use Simple Sentences Circle the simple sentence below. Then write three simple sentences of your own.

1. The skeleton protects the soft body parts inside the body.

2. When the exoskeleton becomes too small, the crab crawls out of it.

3. _____

_____

4. _____

_____

5. _____

_____

Students write routinely for a range of tasks, purposes, and audiences.
Students practice various conventions of standard English.

Name _____

DIRECTIONS Use each word below in a sentence.

affect   flexible   hinge

_____

_____

_____

_____

_____

Write in Response to Reading

DIRECTIONS Reread p. 9 of *Skeletons Inside and Out*. Write several sentences about the different types of joints, explaining their function and purpose. Note which text features helped you identify the function and purpose.

_____

_____

_____

_____

_____

Students show contextual understanding of Benchmark Vocabulary. Students write routinely for a range of tasks, purposes, and audiences.

Name _____

DIRECTIONS Using evidence from the text, answer the following questions about pp. 6–10 from *Skeletons Inside and Out*.

1. What is the genre of this selection? How do you know?

   _____

   _____

2. Reread pp. 6–7. What kinds of text features are on these pages?

   _____

   _____

3. What is the purpose of the sidebar on p. 6?

   _____

   _____

4. What ideas are included on pp. 8–9?

   _____

   _____

5. How is a new idea presented on these pages?

   _____

   _____

Students analyze and respond to literary and informational text.

Name _____

DIRECTIONS Reread pp. 8–9 of *Skeletons Inside and Out*. Write a brief informative paragraph about spines, bones, and joints. Focus on establishing your purpose for writing. Be sure to provide facts, details, and a visual in order to inform readers.

_____

_____

_____

_____

_____

Conventions

Compound Sentences For questions 1 and 2, use *and, or, but,* or *so* to combine each sentence. For questions 3 and 4, write *and, or, but,* or *so* in the blank to complete each sentence.

1. Humans walk on two legs. The spine is vertical.

_____

_____

2. You may call them bugs. Spiders and scorpions aren't insects.

_____

_____

3. It's important to study, _____ it helps to read carefully.

4. The sky is getting dark, _____ we'll examine the skeleton tomorrow.

Students write routinely for a range of tasks, purposes, and audiences.
Students practice various conventions of standard English.

Name _____

DIRECTIONS Use each word in a sentence.

survive   spongy   ability

_____

_____

_____

_____

_____

_____

Write in Response to Reading

DIRECTIONS Reread p. 12 of *Skeletons Inside and Out*. Write several sentences stating whether chimpanzees are more like cats or more like humans. State your opinion and support it using text evidence and visuals from the text.

_____

_____

_____

_____

Students show contextual understanding of Benchmark Vocabulary. Students write routinely for a range of tasks, purposes, and audiences.

What Did You Say?

How would you communicate if you couldn't speak, use sign language, or grab the closest hand-held device and start texting? In baseball, players and coaches often use hand signals to communicate about stealing a base, hitting the ball into left field, or throwing a fastball. What do animals do? Animals can't speak, so they use visuals, sounds, and touch to communicate. You may be wondering what an animal possibly has to say—a lot actually!

Peacocks and fireflies use visuals to attract mates. Male peacocks are known for their beautiful, colorful feathers. They fan out their feathers and parade in front of females. Male fireflies light their fire, so to speak. They use light to attract females by signaling to them. Females respond by flashing their own light. Light and color are visuals that allow these animals to communicate.

Under the sea and in the sky, whales and birds communicate using sound. Whales, such as the humpback whale, use sounds called phonations, which are too low or too high for humans to hear. Whales produce these sounds to keep in contact with other whales. The whale sounds travel long distance and then some. They can reach whales that may be swimming as many as 50 miles (80 kilometers) away. Ponder that!

The songs and calls that birds make can be beautiful and melodic. But did you know that birdsong is their way or means to communicate? Birds sing and call for many reasons. They may sing to attract a mate or call to warn off a predator. They may even sing because they are annoyed. Consider this technique the next time someone is bothering you!

Elephants use sound to communicate, but they also use touch. A mother elephant uses her trunk to gently stroke her calf or to discipline it. Two elephants greet each other with their trunks. They place the tip of the trunk in the other's mouth. This greeting can be translated into saying, "Hello!"

Think of how these animals communicate the next time you need to share information with someone. Instead of speaking, using sign language, or texting, try something unique and act like a peacock!

Students read text closely to determine what the text says.

Name _____

Gather Evidence Circle the names of two animals mentioned in the text. Briefly explain how they communicate to other animals without using words.

Gather Evidence: Extend Your Ideas Focusing on the animals you identified, tell what kind of message these animals might be communicating to another animal.

_____

Ask Questions Draw a box around the name of one animal mentioned in the text. Write three questions you want to research to learn more about this animal's communication method.

Ask Questions: Extend Your Ideas Write additional questions you could ask about how other animals communicate.

_____

Make Your Case Underline the main idea the writer was trying to share. List several details from the text that support this idea.

Make Your Case: Extend Your Ideas Briefly explain how communication is important to animals.

_____

_____

_____

Students read text closely to determine what the text says.

DIRECTIONS Write a paragraph that compares and contrasts the skeletons of two animals you have read about in this section of the text. Use linking words and phrases as you give facts about how the skeletons are similar and different.

_____

_____

_____

_____

_____

_____

Conventions

Complete Sentences Correctly punctuate the sentences below.

1. Like humans chimpanzees are able to pick up many different things with their hands.

2. The ribs of the skeleton protect some of the bodys most important organs.

3. You wouldnt be able to stand up sit down run or walk without bones.

4. The hard covering over each leg is divided into seven segments or parts.

5. Insects like ladybugs have bodies with three main parts and six walking legs.

Students write routinely for a range of tasks, purposes, and audiences. Students practice various conventions of standard English.

Name _____

DIRECTIONS Use each word in a sentence.

vary   hollow

_____

_____

_____

_____

DIRECTIONS Reread the second paragraph on p. 15 of *Skeletons Inside and Out*. Write a short paragraph that explains how bats' bones help them survive.

_____

_____

_____

_____

Students show contextual understanding of Benchmark Vocabulary. Students write routinely for a range of tasks, purposes, and audiences.

DIRECTIONS Write an informative/explanatory paragraph summarizing information from *Skeletons Inside and Out*. Choose to write about either bat skeletons or bird skeletons. Your paragraph should include an illustration based on the one found in the text. Include labels pointing to key features of the illustration.

_____

_____

_____

_____

_____

Conventions

Understand and Use Pronouns Circle the pronoun in the sentences below and underline the noun that it replaces. Then write your own pair of sentences, circling the pronoun and underlining the noun that it replaces.

1. Birds have beaks for eating and grasping food. They also have large sternums, or breastbones.

2. The zoologist handled the skeleton carefully. Then he returned the bones to the shelf.

3. Samantha loved to read about chimpanzees. She spent many evenings studying in the library.

4. Nerves carry information from the body to the brain. They also carry commands from the brain to parts of the body.

5. _____

_____

Students write routinely for a range of tasks, purposes, and audiences. Students practice various conventions of standard English.

Name _____

DIRECTIONS Use each word in a sentence.

sturdy   fossils   ancient   detach

_____

_____

_____

_____

_____

_____

_____

Write in Response to Reading

DIRECTIONS Reread the second paragraph on p. 19 of *Skeletons Inside and Out*. Write a short paragraph that gives your description of a salamander's skeleton. Include text evidence and vivid words in your description.

_____

_____

_____

_____

Students show contextual understanding of Benchmark Vocabulary. Students write routinely for a range of tasks, purposes, and audiences.

Name _____

DIRECTIONS Reread pp. 17–19 of *Skeletons Inside and Out*, and focus on alliteration, or words that begin with the same sound.

1. Read the first paragraph on page 17. What phrase in the paragraph is an example of alliteration?

   _____

   _____

2. Read the caption on page 17 and identify the example of alliteration. What does this figurative language describe?

   _____

   _____

3. Read the paragraph on page 18. Write an example of alliteration used there.

   _____

   _____

4. Read the first paragraph on page 19. Name one example of alliteration in the paragraph and tell what it helps you understand.

   _____

   _____

5. Use alliteration to compare and contrast two of the animals you read about on pages 17–19.

   _____

   _____

   _____

Students analyze and respond to literary and informational text.

Name _____

DIRECTIONS Choose an animal to research using two or three reputable sources. Take notes. After researching, write and illustrate a paragraph about your topic, paraphrasing or directly quoting sources and providing citations as needed.

_____

_____

_____

_____

Conventions

Antecedent-Pronoun Agreement Correct the antecedent-pronoun agreement in the sentences below.

1. Every amphibian has an endoskeleton that helps them move in and out of water.

_____

_____

2. A snake's vertebrae allow them to move in many different directions.

_____

_____

3. Crocodiles use its powerful jaws and strong teeth to capture prey.

_____

_____

Students write routinely for a range of tasks, purposes, and audiences. Students practice various conventions of standard English.

Synonyms, Antonyms

Word Bank

music	musician	select	selection	sign
signal	part	partial	haste	hasten
protect	protection	magic	magician	resign
resignation	electric	electrician	condemn	condemnation

Antonyms Write the list word that has the opposite or nearly opposite meaning.

1. whole

1. _____

2. do not choose

2. _____

3. harm

3. _____

4. recommendation

4. _____

5. delay

5. _____

Synonyms Write the list word that has the same or nearly the same meaning.

6. incomplete

6. _____

7. indicator

7. _____

8. security

8. _____

9. choice

9. _____

10. denounce

10. _____

Students apply grade-level phonics and word analysis skills.

Name _____

DIRECTIONS Use the word below in a sentence.

tissue

_____

_____

DIRECTIONS Reread pp. 20–24 of *Skeletons Inside and Out*. Choose one sea creature and one other animal you have read about in this book. Write an expository paragraph comparing and contrasting the skeletons of the two animals. Use key details from the text to support your response.

_____

_____

_____

_____

Students show contextual understanding of Benchmark Vocabulary. Students write routinely for a range of tasks, purposes, and audiences.

Name _____

DIRECTIONS Write an informative/explanatory paragraph about an animal, flower, or plant you have observed. Develop your topic with concrete details. Remember to include vivid, specific language that will paint a picture in the reader's mind.

_____

_____

_____

_____

_____

_____

Conventions

Use Adjectives to Compare Write the correct form of the adjective in each sentence below.

1. Stingrays are _____ creatures than sharks. (gentle)

2. Giraffes' long legs and necks make them the _____ mammals in the world. (tall)

3. Does an elephant have _____ bones than a bat? (strong)

4. I heard that ravens are the _____ birds on Earth. (smart)

5. Which animal can make the _____ jump, a frog, a kangaroo, or a chimpanzee? (high)

Students write routinely for a range of tasks, purposes, and audiences. Students practice various conventions of standard English.

Name _____

DIRECTIONS Use each word in a sentence.

segments   armor

_____

_____

_____

_____

DIRECTIONS Reread pp. 25–29 of *Skeletons Inside and Out*. Write several sentences explaining whether you think it is better to have an endoskeleton or an exoskeleton. State your opinion and support it with text evidence.

_____

_____

_____

_____

Students show contextual understanding of Benchmark Vocabulary. Students write routinely for a range of tasks, purposes, and audiences.

Name _____

DIRECTIONS Identify an animal with an exoskeleton to research, and write a one-page informative/explanatory text about this animal. As you write about the animal, remember to group related information in paragraphs. Be sure that each paragraph has a main idea and supporting details. Remember that all details within a paragraph should relate to each other.

_____

_____

_____

_____

_____

_____

Conventions

Sentence Fragments Turn the sentence fragments below into complete sentences. Use information from pp. 25–29 of *Skeletons Inside and Out* to help you.

1. A ladybug has _____

2. Almost half of crocodile vertebrae _____

3. _____ because it has both an endoskeleton and an exoskeleton.

4. To easily move fast, a salamander _____

5. _____ has an amazing ability to jump.

Students write routinely for a range of tasks, purposes, and audiences. Students practice various conventions of standard English.

Name _____

DIRECTIONS Use each word in a sentence.

survive   ability

_____
_____
_____
_____

Write in Response to Reading

DIRECTIONS Look through *Skeletons Inside and Out*, and select an animal that interests you. Write a description of how the animal moves and how its skeleton is important to that movement. Use text evidence to support your response.

_____
_____
_____
_____
_____

Students show contextual understanding of Benchmark Vocabulary. Students write routinely for a range of tasks, purposes, and audiences.

Name _____

DIRECTIONS Using evidence from the text, answer the following
questions about pp. 30–32 from *Skeletons Inside and Out*.

1. What is the author's purpose for including page 30?

_____

_____

2. What's the author's purpose for including an index?

_____

_____

3. Pick one topic from the index. Record the page numbers, reread those
   sections, and include something you learned from that section.

_____

_____

4. Turn to the page about the sea urchin. What was the author's purpose
   for including a picture of it?

_____

_____

5. Turn to the page about jellyfish. Why do you think the author
   included this sidebar?

_____

_____

Students analyze and respond to literary and
informational text.

Name _____

DIRECTIONS Create an infographic to show readers how to take care of a pet. You should focus on establishing a clear purpose for your writing. Begin by locating information about your topic, and then assemble it. Remember that the manner in which you arrange your information will determine whether your purpose is clearly communicated.

_____

_____

_____

_____

_____

_____

Conventions

Run-On Sentences Correct the run-on sentences below.

1. Skeletons support the body's weight they protect the organs of the body, such as the brain.

_____

2. To move fast, a salamander sways its body to leap, it flexes and straightens its tail.

_____

3. Kangaroos' skeletons help them stay upright as they jump along, they use their tails for balance.

_____

Students write routinely for a range of tasks, purposes, and audiences. Students practice various conventions of standard English.

Name _____

DIRECTIONS Use each word in a sentence.

internal   contract   shield   rigid

_____

_____

_____

_____

_____

_____

_____

Write in Response to Reading

DIRECTIONS Reread pp. 16–18 of *Movers and Shapers*. Choose a section of text, such as "Bone marrow," and explain how the heading, text, and visuals support the main idea of that section.

_____

_____

_____

_____

_____

Students show contextual understanding of Benchmark Vocabulary. Students write routinely for a range of tasks, purposes, and audiences.

Name _____

DIRECTIONS Research and write an informative/explanatory paragraph about a topic from the text—such as muscles, bones, or bone marrow. Your paragraph should be accurate and precise, and contain vivid, specific language and domain-specific vocabulary.

_____

_____

_____

_____

_____

_____

Conventions

Complete Sentences Identify the sentences below as either a fragment, a run-on, or a complete sentence.

1. Spine made up of vertebrae. _____

2. The giraffe is the largest known mammal on Earth. _____

3. Bones are made of living cells and can change over time this is why tight shoes can be harmful. _____

4. The fluid in between cartilage. _____

5. Blood vessels supply your body's cells with food and energy. _____

Students write routinely for a range of tasks, purposes, and audiences. Students practice various conventions of standard English.

Lesson 10

Name _____

DIRECTIONS Use each word in a sentence.

rotates   pivot   artificial   chambers

_____

_____

_____

_____

_____

_____

_____

_____

DIRECTIONS Reread pp. 20–21 of *Movers and Shapers*. Write several sentences explaining which joints the woman on pp. 20–21 is using to jump and how each type of joint helps her make these motions. Use evidence from the text to support your answer.

_____

_____

_____

_____

_____

Students show contextual understanding of Benchmark Vocabulary. Students write routinely for a range of tasks, purposes, and audiences.

Name _____

Using evidence from the text, answer the following questions about pp. 20–25 from *Movers and Shapers*.

1. What does the text say about hinge joints on p. 20?

_____

_____

2. What are some everyday things that have hinges?

_____

_____

3. Make an inference. How do everyday examples help you understand that hinge joints can only move in one direction?

_____

_____

4. What does the text say about the thumb joint on p. 21?

_____

_____

5. What details does the text provide about gripping objects?

_____

_____

6. Try picking up several objects in the classroom. Then make an inference about the saddle joint. How does it help you grip objects?

_____

_____

Students analyze and respond to literary and informational text.

Name _____

DIRECTIONS Write a one-page informative/explanatory text about the muscles and joints you use when you play your favorite sport. Remember to group related information in paragraphs and to be sure that each paragraph contains a main idea and supporting details.

_____

_____

_____

_____

_____

_____

_____

_____

_____

Conventions

Correct Fragments Correct the sentence fragments below using information from pp. 20–25 of *Movers & Shapers*.

1. Flexibility allows you to _____

2. The elbow is an example of _____

3. Some people have extremely flexible _____

4. Your nose and voice box, which is the bumpy part in your neck,

   _____

5. The most movable of all joints _____

Students write routinely for a range of tasks, purposes, and audiences. Students practice various conventions of standard English.

Prefixes *un–*, *in–*

Word Bank

unavailable	uncertain	incomplete	unlikely	unfair
inconsistent	unaware	infinite	indefinite	indirect
unopened	inability	unimportant	unlisted	indecent
unable	inexact	unsolved	uncover	unsuspecting

Add Prefixes Write the list word that can replace the underlined words.

1. The mystery of the missing book is still <u>not solved</u>. 1. _____

2. The team's performance was <u>not consistent</u>. 2. _____

3. Our calculations were <u>not exact</u>. 3. _____

4. It's seven o'clock, and my homework is still <u>not complete</u>. 4. _____

5. It's <u>not likely</u> that we'll see a flying elephant anytime soon. 5. _____

6. The outcome of the contest is still <u>not certain</u>. 6. _____

Synonyms Write a list word that has the same or almost the same meaning as the clues.

7. not suspicious 7. _____

8. not direct 8. _____

9. expose 9. _____

10. busy 10. _____

11. unjust 11. _____

12. improper 12. _____

13. not finished 13. _____

14. not expected 14. _____

15. lack of skill 15. _____

Students apply grade-level phonics and word analysis skills.

Name _____

DIRECTIONS Use each word in a sentence.

vessels   knitted   fused   atlas

_____

_____

_____

_____

_____

_____

_____

Write in Response to Reading

DIRECTIONS Write several sentences giving your opinion about what you think is the most important group of bones in the human body. Use details and domain-specific vocabulary from *Movers and Shapers* to support your opinion.

_____

_____

_____

_____

_____

Students show contextual understanding of Benchmark Vocabulary. Students write routinely for a range of tasks, purposes, and audiences.

Name _____

DIRECTIONS Write a descriptive paragraph using domain-specific vocabulary and vivid, specific language to describe the bones and muscles used by athletes playing a particular sport. Be sure to include facts, definitions, and concrete details supported by your research.

_____

_____

_____

_____

_____

_____

Conventions

Modal Auxiliaries Underline the auxiliary verb in the sentences below. Then write two of your own sentences using auxiliary verbs.

1. If you twist your ankle suddenly, you may tear and stretch the ligaments in the ankle joints.

2. I can study bones and joints in my free time.

3. The research group might receive a grant from the foundation.

4. _____

_____

5. _____

_____

Students write routinely for a range of tasks, purposes, and audiences. Students practice various conventions of standard English.

Name _____

DIRECTIONS Use each word in a sentence.

framework   detach   contract   chambers

_____

_____

_____

_____

_____

_____

_____

**Write in
Response to
Reading**

DIRECTIONS Write several sentences explaining how the spine works
with joints to help the human body move. Use details from *Skeletons
Inside and Out* and *Movers and Shapers* to support your answer.

_____

_____

_____

_____

_____

Students show contextual understanding
of Benchmark Vocabulary. Students write
routinely for a range of tasks, purposes, and
audiences.

Name _____

DIRECTIONS Using evidence from the text, answer the following questions about pp. 6–10 of *Skeletons Inside and Out* and pp. 16–19 of *Movers and Shapers*.

1. Reread p. 6 of *Skeletons Inside and Out*. What do bones need in order to grow?

   _____

   _____

2. Reread pp. 7–8 of *Skeletons Inside and Out*. Choose two different bones and explain their purpose.

   _____

   _____

3. Why is the spine so important? What does it protect?

   _____

   _____

4. Reread pp. 16–17 of *Movers and Shapers*. What is compact bone? What is it made of?

   _____

   _____

5. What is spongy bone? How is it different from compact bone?

   _____

   _____

Students analyze and respond to literary and informational text.

Name _____

DIRECTIONS Identify a sport or other athletic activity and describe the functioning of bones and muscles during that activity. You should do prewriting and planning in order to write a one-page informative text describing the bones' and muscles' functioning. Use a graphic organizer, such as a sequence chart, to help plan your writing.

_____

_____

_____

_____

_____

_____

Conventions

Prepositional Phrases Underline the prepositional phrase in the sentences below. Then write two of your own sentences using prepositional phrases.

1. The subject of the text is muscles and bones.

2. I left the skeletal sample with my colleague.

3. The slippery coating around the joints is called cartilage.

4. _____

   _____

5. _____

   _____

Students write routinely for a range of tasks, purposes, and audiences. Students practice various conventions of standard English.

Name _____

DIRECTIONS Use each word in a sentence.

mission   legendary   reputation   portray   remains

_____

_____

_____

_____

_____

_____

_____

_____

**Write in
Response to
Reading**

DIRECTIONS Write several sentences telling whether or not you think it
is a good idea to study artifacts and human remains to learn about the past.
Explain why or why not. Use details from "King of the Parking Lot" to
support your opinion.

_____

_____

_____

_____

_____

Students show contextual understanding
of Benchmark Vocabulary. Students write
routinely for a range of tasks, purposes,
and audiences.

Name _____

Adapting to Survive

If you have ever moved to a new town or city or even another country, you might know how it feels to have to adapt to your new surroundings. Animals face similar challenges. However, their true test is whether they can survive in their environment or become another animal's lunch!

Adaptations are what animals use to help them survive. As their surroundings change, many animals use adaptations to become better suited for their new homes. Did that leaf just move? A leaf frog uses an adaptation called camouflage to blend into its surroundings. Camouflage helps animals survive. An animal's coloring or shape can help it hide in plain sight. Predators have a hard time spying camouflaged animals.

However, predators also use camouflage to sneak up on prey. Leopards' spots help them blend into their surroundings. They wait for their prey in shadows or in shaded grass. Their prey may not notice the leopard until it is too late.

Mimicry is another survival adaptation. Mimicry is when an animal looks like, or copies, another living thing or an object. Some animals are harmless, so they mimic dangerous animals. When an animal uses mimicry, it tricks predators into not wanting to eat it for dinner. For example, the underside of an owl butterfly's wing has a large spot. It looks like an owl's eye. When predators see the butterfly, they are scared off. Without that spot, they might try to pursue the butterfly. The predators are fooled into thinking the butterfly is an owl. Owls might attack them if provoked. By looking like this animal, owl butterflies have a better chance of surviving.

Predators also use mimicry to attract prey. An alligator snapping turtle has a tongue that looks like a juicy worm. Fish like to eat worms, and snapping turtles like to eat fish! The snapping turtles can use their tongues to catch fish. Chomp!

If you were thinking that camouflage might help you to hide from your next chore or homework assignment, you are out of luck. Camouflage and mimicry are adaptations that help animals, not humans, survive. Next time you are outside see what luck you might have finding a camouflaged animal. If you spy one, consider yourself lucky and a great sleuth!

Students read text closely to determine what the text says.

Name _____

Gather Evidence Circle ways that camouflage and mimicry are alike, and underline ways they are different. List some of the similarities and differences.

_____

_____

Gather Evidence: Extend Your Ideas Choose one animal from the text that uses camouflage and one animal that uses mimicry, and tell how each animal uses the adaptation.

_____

_____

Ask Questions Draw a box around the name of one animal mentioned in the text that uses mimicry or camouflage. Write an interesting question about this animal.

_____

Ask Questions: Extend Your Ideas Write additional questions you could ask about other animals mentioned in the text.

_____

Make Your Case Bracket reasons that the writer gives to support the idea that animals use mimicry to survive. Briefly describe the reasons.

Make Your Case: Extend Your Ideas Briefly explain how predators and prey can each use mimicry to their advantage.

_____

_____

_____

Students read text closely to determine what the text says.

Name _____

DIRECTIONS Craft an introductory paragraph for your informative/ explanatory writing from Lesson 12. Remember to clearly establish a topic and to use an effective strategy to gain the attention of readers. Be sure to explain the importance of your topic.

_____

_____

_____

_____

_____

_____

Conventions

Nouns Underline the proper noun and circle one common noun in the following sentences.

1. William Shakespeare wrote the play in 1592.

2. However, there was no body or skeleton of Richard III anywhere to be found.

3. This map showed a possible location of the Greyfriars Church.

4. This group studies everything about King Richard III.

5. Philippa raised money and got a license to start an excavation to dig.

Students write routinely for a range of tasks, purposes, and audiences. Students practice various conventions of standard English.

Name _____

DIRECTIONS Use each word in a sentence.

trenches   deformed   fragile

_____

_____

_____

_____

_____

**Write in
Response to
Reading**

DIRECTIONS Choose a paragraph from pp. 38–40 of "King of the
Parking Lot" to examine. Write an informational paragraph summarizing
the most important information found in this section of the text. Include
only key details that support the main idea.

_____

_____

_____

_____

Students show contextual understanding
of Benchmark Vocabulary. Students write
routinely for a range of tasks, purposes,
and audiences.

Name _____

DIRECTIONS Using evidence from the text, answer the following questions about the section "What They Found" in "King of the Parking Lot."

1. Reread the first three paragraphs of the section "What They Found." What is the main idea of the first paragraph? What details support the main idea?

_____

_____

2. What is the main idea of the second paragraph? What details support the main idea?

_____

_____

3. What is the main idea of the third paragraph? What details support the main idea?

_____

_____

4. Summarize these three paragraphs using the most important information.

_____

_____

_____

_____

Students analyze and respond to literary and informational text.

Name _____

DIRECTIONS Revisit the informative/explanatory text you began working on in Lessons 12 and 13. Create an infographic to support information in your text. Consider how the visuals and text will work together to make complex information clear for readers. Consult the models in the text as you create your visual.

_____

_____

_____

_____

_____

Conventions

Form and Use Progressive Verb Tenses Underline the progressive verb tense in the sentences below. Then write two of your own sentences using progressive verb tenses.

1. Modern scientists are studying people who lived long ago.

2. The archaeologists will be digging at the site tomorrow.

3. The researcher was frantically trying to piece together the evidence needed to prove her theory.

4. _____

_____

5. _____

_____

Students write routinely for a range of tasks, purposes, and audiences. Students practice various conventions of standard English.

Name _____

DIRECTIONS Use each word in a sentence.

depiction   ancestors   descendants   reconstruction

_____

_____

_____

_____

_____

_____

_____

**Write in
Response to
Reading**

DIRECTIONS Reread pp. 41–44 of "The King of the Parking Lot."
Write several sentences describing your opinion about how successful you
think Philippa Langley's search was. Include examples from the text to
support your ideas.

_____

_____

_____

_____

_____

Students show contextual understanding
of Benchmark Vocabulary. Students write
routinely for a range of tasks, purposes, and
audiences.

Name _____

DIRECTIONS Revise the informative/explanatory writing you drafted in Lessons 12, 13, and 14. Your writing should include an introduction paragraph that establishes your purpose, body paragraphs that present important information and details, and a conclusion paragraph that sums up the most significant points of your piece. Remember to use linking words and phrases to connect ideas and details.

_____

_____

_____

_____

_____

_____

Conventions

Modal Auxiliaries Write your own sentences below using modal auxiliaries.

1. _____

_____

2. _____

_____

3. _____

_____

4. _____

_____

Students write routinely for a range of tasks, purposes, and audiences. Students practice various conventions of standard English.

Name _____

Words from Other Languages

Word Bank

khaki	hula	banana	ballet	waltz
tomato	yogurt	macaroni	polka	koala
barbecue	buffet	stampede	karate	

Word Histories Write a list word for each description.

1. This is French for a table full of different foods. 1. _____

2. Many students practice this Japanese form of self-defense. 2. _____

3. Native Americans introduced this fruit to the settlers. 3. _____

4. This is a Turkish treat made from milk. 4. _____

5. This Polynesian dance is usually performed in a grass skirt. 5. _____

6. This is a Spanish word for a large group of running buffaloes or horses. 6. _____

7. Although it has a French name, this dance form started in Russia. 7. _____

8. This furry animal has kept its Australian name. 8. _____

9. Soldiers wear this yellowish brown fabric named by the Persians and Hindus so they can't be easily seen. 9. _____

10. This partner dance means "to turn" in German. 10. _____

11. This is an Italian name for a well-known pasta. 11. _____

12. The Spanish and Portuguese used the same name for this yellow fruit. 12. _____

13. A Native American word is used to name this kind of outside cooking. 13. _____

14. This Polish dance is very lively. 14. _____

Students apply grade-level phonics and word analysis skills.

Name _____

DIRECTIONS Use each word in a sentence.

expand   ancient   mission   reputation

_____

_____

_____

_____

_____

_____

_____

DIRECTIONS Write a paragraph that compares the purpose of *Skeletons Inside and Out* with the purpose of "King of the Parking Lot." Include details from both texts to support your ideas.

_____

_____

_____

_____

_____

Students show contextual understanding of Benchmark Vocabulary. Students write routinely for a range of tasks, purposes, and audiences.

Name _____

DIRECTIONS Edit and proofread your informative/explanatory draft. Be sure that you have included all relevant information and deleted any irrelevant information. Check that you have spelled words correctly and used proper punctuation and capitalization.

_____

_____

_____

_____

_____

_____

Conventions

Correctly Use Frequently Confused Words Read each sentence. Cross out the misspelled word, and write the corrected word on the line.

1. Muscles move the body because they are attached two the skeleton.

_____

2. Wherever too or more bones meet, you will find a joint.

_____

3. There equipment was hauled into the parking lot on a large truck.

_____

4. Philippa waited silently for the carbon dating results. Everyone else did two.

_____

Students write routinely for a range of tasks, purposes, and audiences. Students practice various conventions of standard English.

Name _____

DIRECTIONS Use each word in a sentence.

    flexible   artificial   fused   reputation   fragile

_____

_____

_____

_____

_____

_____

_____

Write in Response to Reading

DIRECTIONS Write several sentences telling whether you think it is better to have a skeleton on the inside of your body, like a human, or on the outside of your body, like a crab. Include details from at least two of the texts you have read to support your ideas.

_____

_____

_____

_____

Students show contextual understanding of Benchmark Vocabulary. Students write routinely for a range of tasks, purposes, and audiences.

Name _____

Using evidence from the text, answer the following questions about *Skeletons Inside and Out, Movers and Shapers,* and "King of the Parking Lot."

1. Both *Skeletons Inside and Out* and *Movers and Shapers* include information about joints. What kinds of images does each text use to show these joints?

   _____

   _____

2. In which text did you learn the most about the human body? Explain your answer using text evidence.

   _____

   _____

3. How are *Skeletons Inside and Out, Movers and Shapers,* and "King of the Parking Lot" similar?

   _____

   _____

   _____

4. How are *Movers and Shapers* and "King of the Parking Lot" different?

   _____

   _____

   _____

Students analyze and respond to literary and informational text.

Name _____

DIRECTIONS Publish and present the revised version of your informative/explanatory writing. Include headings and visuals to support your writing. Be sure that you have adequately planned your presentation, added supporting information, and altered your writing as necessary. Then practice presenting your writing to a partner.

_____

_____

_____

_____

_____

_____

Conventions

Using a Dictionary Read each sentence. Then write the definition of the word in bold on the lines below. Use a dictionary as a reference.

1. As a modern-day **screenwriter** and history fan, Philippa's favorite topic to study is Richard III, one of the most famous kings in England's history.

   Definition: _____

2. Richard III's ancestors were traced back over 17 generations to two **descendants** alive today in Canada.

   Definition: _____

3. Once the king's identity was **confirmed**, one last specialist was called in.

   Definition: _____

Students write routinely for a range of tasks, purposes, and audiences. Students practice various conventions of standard English.

Name _____

DIRECTIONS Use each word in a sentence.

segments   internal   rigid   legendary   depiction

_____

_____

_____

_____

_____

_____

_____

**Write in
Response to
Reading**

DIRECTIONS Compare the language used in *Skeletons Inside and Out,
Movers and Shapers,* and "King of the Parking Lot." Use an example from
each text to support your answer.

_____

_____

_____

_____

Students show contextual understanding
of Benchmark Vocabulary. Students write
routinely for a range of tasks, purposes, and
audiences.

Name _____

DIRECTIONS Write three paragraphs comparing *Skeletons Inside and Out* and "Movers and Shapers." Your third paragraph should be a strong conclusion that restates your main opinion clearly and concisely. Include a clincher to make your conclusion more engaging. Remember that a clincher must relate to the topic, but can also help readers consider your topic in a new way.

_____

_____

_____

_____

_____

_____

_____

Conventions

Review Using Frequently Confused Words Read each sentence. Cross out the misspelled word, and write the correct word on the line.

1. There endoskeletons help them move around on land and sometimes in water.

   _____

2. Their remarkable reptiles because they have both endoskeletons and exoskeletons.

   _____

3. They're are 206 bones in an adult's skeleton.

   _____

Students write routinely for a range of tasks, purposes, and audiences. Students practice various conventions of standard English.

Latin Prefixes *dis-*, *re-*, *non-*

Word Bank

distrust	disrespect	nonprofit	rebound
discontinue	reunion	repack	nonstick
remove	disobey	discount	disrepair
nonsense	nonfiction	disobey	reseal

Add Prefixes Write the list word that can replace the underlined words.

1. We decided to <u>not continue</u> the newspaper delivery.   1. _____

2. I didn't want to <u>pack again</u>.   2. _____

3. He didn't want to <u>seal again</u> his patio this winter.   3. _____

4. Jim loved cooking with his <u>not stick</u> pans.   4. _____

5. The puppy does not mean to <u>not obey</u>.   5. _____

6. Elaine worked for a <u>not profit</u> organization.   6. _____

7. His teacher didn't want to <u>not count</u> his efforts.   7. _____

8. We <u>do not trust</u> people who do not tell the truth.   8. _____

9. The story he told was <u>not sense</u>.   9. _____

Missing Words Write the list word that best completes each sentence.

10. Textbooks and biographies are examples of ___.   10. _____

11. My friends from kindergarten and I got together for a ___.   11. _____

12. The old house has fallen into ___.   12. _____

13. My suitcase was too full so I had to ___ it.   13. _____

14. The forward got the ___ and made a basket.   14. _____

15. I don't mean any ___, but I don't agree with your opinion.   15. _____

16. A ___ pan is easy to clean.   16. _____

Students apply grade-level phonics and word analysis skills.

DIRECTIONS Use each word in a sentence.

wounds   tastier   preserve   mined

_____

_____

_____

_____

DIRECTIONS Reread pp. 11–13 of *Why the Sea Is Salty*. What are some dangers the villagers face when they travel to the giant's island? Use evidence from the text to support your answer.

_____

_____

_____

_____

Students show contextual understanding of Benchmark Vocabulary. Students write routinely for a range of tasks, purposes, and audiences.

Name _____

DIRECTIONS Reread pp. 5–8 of *Why the Sea Is Salty*. Write a paragraph in which you establish a narrative situation. This will be the opening paragraph for your own narrative.

_____

_____

_____

_____

_____

Conventions

Adjectives Write your own sentences using vivid adjectives on the lines below.

1. _____

_____

2. _____

_____

3. _____

_____

4. _____

_____

Students write routinely for a range of tasks, purposes, and audiences. Students practice various conventions of standard English.

Name _____

DIRECTIONS Use each word in a sentence.

rough   chamber   crouching

_____

_____

_____

_____

Write in Response to Reading

DIRECTIONS Reread pp. 15–16 of *Why the Sea Is Salty*. Why does the father let his son go to the giant's island with him? Use details from the text to support your answer.

_____

_____

_____

_____

_____

Students show contextual understanding of Benchmark Vocabulary. Students write routinely for a range of tasks, purposes, and audiences.

Name _____

DIRECTIONS Using evidence from the text, answer the following questions about pp. 14–21 from *Why the Sea Is Salty*.

1. Reread the final paragraph on p. 18. Why is the giant disappointed?

   _____

   _____

2. Reread p. 20. What does the child think about that makes him nervous?

   _____

   _____

3. How do you know?

   _____

   _____

   _____

4. Reread p. 21. Why is the child's body sore?

   _____

   _____

5. How do you know?

   _____

   _____

   _____

Students analyze and respond to literary and informational text.

Name _____

DIRECTIONS Write a brief narrative that involves an experience with nature. Your narrative should set up a situation in nature, outline key events of the plot, and introduce the setting and characters. Revisit the text to help you.

_____

_____

_____

_____

_____

Conventions

Order Adjectives Write sentences that describe characters from pp. 14–21 of *Why the Sea Is Salty*. Remember to arrange your adjectives in the proper order. Revisit the text to help you.

1. _____

_____

2. _____

_____

3. _____

_____

4. _____

_____

Students write routinely for a range of tasks, purposes, and audiences. Students practice various conventions of standard English.

Lesson 3

Name _____

DIRECTIONS Use each word in a sentence.

measuring   puzzled   eagerly

_____

_____

_____

_____

Write in Response to Reading

DIRECTIONS Reread the final paragraph on p. 28 of *Why the Sea Is Salty*. How would this paragraph be different if it were written in the first-person? Use details from the text to support your answer.

_____

_____

_____

_____

Students show contextual understanding of Benchmark Vocabulary. Students write routinely for a range of tasks, purposes, and audiences.

Name _____

Cahokia: The Mystery Behind an Ancient City

Hundreds of years before Columbus landed in the New World, there was a complex culture in southern Illinois. People settled in the rich floodplain near present-day St. Louis beginning about A.D. 700. Over the centuries, they built a planned city. It was later named Cahokia (kuh HO key uh). Between the years 1050 and 1200, the city had between 10,000 and 20,000 people living there.

What was the daily life like at Cahokia? There are no written records to tell us. Scientists have searched for clues as they have dug at the site of this ancient city. They have found pottery, buildings, and burial grounds.

More than 120 earthen pyramids, known as mounds, have been discovered. The largest mound has a base that covers more than 14 acres. It would have been more than ten stories tall! It may have required more than about 14 million baskets of soil to build it. Imagine a powerful leader ordering workers to carry all those baskets, one at a time. Between the mounds, there are large plazas where people may have gathered and played sports.

What were the mounds used for? A large temple or palace on the highest mound may have been where the high priest lived. Homes or burial grounds may have been located in some of the mounds. Scientists have found a circle of cedar posts that may have been used like a calendar. The Cahokian people likely studied the movement of the sun and stars.

Cahokian artifacts that were found hundreds of miles away from Cahokia suggest that a large trade network was in place. Scientists are not certain, but some think that Cahokia may have been the center of the Mississippian culture.

What happened to the Cahokian people? Did disease kill them? Were they forced to move? No one really knows. Perhaps their resources ran out. Why should we care about this long-lost city? Understanding how great civilizations rose and fell may help us to learn from their failures. It may help to ensure the survival of our very own culture.

Students read text closely to determine what the text says.

Name _____

Gather Evidence Circle three statements that provide text evidence to explain why mounds provide valuable information about the Cahokian culture. Briefly explain why each statement is important in providing text evidence.

Gather Evidence: Extend Your Ideas Think about the value of mounds to the Cahokian culture. Why do you think the Cahokians might have wanted to be at a higher level than the flat ground?

_____

_____

_____

Ask Questions Draw a box around one statement in the text about Cahokia. Write three questions you want to research to learn more about this information.

Ask Questions: Extend Your Ideas Write two additional questions you would like to ask about mounds built by the Cahokians.

_____

_____

Make Your Case Underline the main idea the writer was trying to share. List several details from the text that support this idea.

Make Your Case: Extend Your Ideas Briefly explain how building mounds can be an important community activity.

_____

_____

Prove It! Have students share their evidence with a classmate.

Students read text closely to determine what the text says.

Name _____

DIRECTIONS Reread pp. 22–31 of *Why the Sea Is Salty.* Pay close attention to the way the author uses dialogue to reveal characters and move the story along. Then write a brief scene involving two characters discussing a problem or an issue.

_____

_____

_____

_____

_____

Quotation Marks Write a brief conversation between two people on the lines below. Remember to use quotation marks correctly.

_____

_____

_____

_____

_____

Students write routinely for a range of tasks, purposes, and audiences. Students practice various conventions of standard English.

Name _____

DIRECTIONS Use each word in a sentence.

wriggled   chuckled   plucked

_____

_____

_____

_____

Write in Response to Reading

DIRECTIONS Reread pp. 38–40 of *Why the Sea Is Salty*. Why does the giant fling the villagers and all of the salt they are carrying into the ocean? Use details from the text to support your answer.

_____

_____

_____

_____

_____

Students show contextual understanding of Benchmark Vocabulary. Students write routinely for a range of tasks, purposes, and audiences.

Name _____

DIRECTIONS Using evidence from the text, answer the following questions about pp. 32–40 from *Why the Sea Is Salty*.

1. List three scenes below that show the text is a Tall Tale. Use details from the text to support your answers.

    Scene 1: _____

    _____

    _____

    Scene 2: _____

    _____

    _____

    Scene 3: _____

    _____

    _____

2. Write a paragraph that explores the lessons found in *Why the Sea Is Salty*. What lessons does the story teach you about life? Use details from the text to support your answer.

    _____

    _____

    _____

    _____

    _____

    _____

    _____

Students analyze and respond to literary and informational text.

Name _____

DIRECTIONS Write a paragraph about the theme of *Why the Sea Is Salty*. Your paragraph should clearly state the theme and your ideas should be supported with relevant details. Include at least two direct quotations from the text to support your answer.

_____

_____

_____

_____

_____

Conventions

Quotation Marks Correctly punctuate the sentences below. Then write two of your own sentences. Remember to use quotation marks correctly.

1. She lulled him into slumber   he said.

2. I must ask them to bring dried squid next time   he thought.

3. Could you please hurry?   he asked.   Ants are biting my feet.

4. _____

_____

5. _____

_____

Students write routinely for a range of tasks, purposes, and audiences. Students practice various conventions of standard English.

Name _____

DIRECTIONS Use each word in a sentence.

legend   mythology   impatiently   squatting

_____

_____

_____

_____

_____

_____

Write in Response to Reading

DIRECTIONS Based on the dialogue on pp. 78–79 of "How the Stars Fell into the Sky," which character understands nature better—First Woman or First Man? Use details from the text to support your answer.

_____

_____

_____

_____

Students show contextual understanding of Benchmark Vocabulary. Students write routinely for a range of tasks, purposes, and audiences.

Name _____

DIRECTIONS Write two paragraphs of a narrative, introducing and developing two characters. Remember that your character's words, thoughts, and actions should make the character come alive for your readers.

_____

_____

_____

_____

_____

_____

Conventions

Simple Sentences Circle the subject and underline the predicate. Then write two of your own sentences. Remember to circle the subject and underline the predicate.

1. The wind will blow them away.

2. Krista and her team were traveling to the island.

3. _____

_____

4. _____

_____

Students write routinely for a range of tasks, purposes, and audiences. Students practice various conventions of standard English.

Name _____

Compound Words

Word Bank

watermelon	homemade	understand	sometimes	shoelace
highway	upstairs	thunderstorm	shortcut	everyone
jellyfish	touchdown	campfire	skateboard	anyway
fireworks	haircut	loudspeaker	laptop	flashlight

Proofread a Schedule Circle the seven misspelled words in the camp schedule, and write them correctly on the lines below.

Monday	Tuesday	Wednesday	Thursday	Friday
Noon Monkey Walk	**11 A.M.** All About Knots: Bring a long shoe lace	**10 A.M.** Fun with Loud Speakers	**9 A.M.** Baking: Learn a shortcut for making a shortcake	**10 A.M** Shave and a Harecut
5 P.M. Homade Fudge Tasting	**5 P.M.** Weather Watch	**3 P.M.** sktaboard Contest	**9 P.M.** Fireworks	**Noon** Upload Camp Pictures
9 P.M. Flashy Flickers: Bring your flashlite		**9 P.M.** Group Meeting: Meet everyon at the campfire		

1. _____ 2. _____ 3. _____

4. _____ 5. _____ 6. _____

7. _____

Proofread Words Circle the list word that is spelled correctly. Write the word.

8. high way   highway   hiway   8. _____

9. understand   under stand   undestand   9. _____

10. somtimes   some times   sometimes   10. _____

Students apply grade-level phonics and word analysis skills.

Name _____

DIRECTIONS Use each word in a sentence.

whine   deliberately   shifting

_____

_____

_____

_____

_____

_____

_____

> **Write in Response to Reading**

DIRECTIONS Reread pp. 82–89 of "How the Stars Fell into the Sky." Based on what you know about Coyote from the details in the text, write a paragraph explaining what Coyote might do next. Use details from the text to support your answer.

_____

_____

_____

_____

_____

Students show contextual understanding of Benchmark Vocabulary. Students write routinely for a range of tasks, purposes, and audiences.

Lesson 6

Name _____

Writing

DIRECTIONS Reread pp. 82–89 of "How the Stars Fell into the Sky." Pay close attention to the words the author uses to describe both Coyote and First Woman. Then write a paragraph about the characters you created in Lesson 5. Use vivid words and precise language to establish a tone and describe your characters' feelings.

_____

_____

_____

_____

_____

Conventions

Complete Sentences Rewrite the fragments below to make complete sentences. Then write your own complete sentence about "How the Stars Fell into the Sky."

1. Walked to the store.

_____

2. were thrown into the night sky

_____

3. High above the village below

_____

4. _____

_____

Students write routinely for a range of tasks, purposes, and audiences. Students practice various conventions of standard English.

Name _____

DIRECTIONS Use each word in a sentence.

grumbled   crouching

_____

_____

_____

_____

Write in Response to Reading

DIRECTIONS Reread pp. 90–95 of "How the Stars Fell into the Sky." Do you think Coyote will follow First Woman's pattern of placing the stars in the sky? Use details from the text to support your answer.

_____

_____

_____

_____

Students show contextual understanding of Benchmark Vocabulary. Students write routinely for a range of tasks, purposes, and audiences.

Name _____

DIRECTIONS Using evidence from the text, answer the following questions about pp. 90–95 from "How the Stars Fell into the Sky."

1. Reread pp. 90–93. What are the characters trying to accomplish in this section?

   _____

   _____

2. Write several sentences about Coyote's point of view.

   _____

   _____

   _____

3. Write several sentences about First Woman's point of view.

   _____

   _____

   _____

   _____

4. Reread pp. 94–95. How do the visuals on these pages support the text?

   _____

   _____

   _____

Students analyze and respond to literary and informational text.

Name _____

DIRECTIONS Write a narrative paragraph that describes a setting of your choice. Choose a time and place that you think would be interesting to set a story in. Use concrete words and phrases to help your readers visualize the setting.

_____

_____

_____

_____

Complete Sentences Rewrite the sentence fragments below to make complete sentences. Then write your own sentence about "How the Stars Fell into the Sky."

1. Stars twinkling above us in the sky.

_____

2. Coyote.

_____

3. could spend all of eternity writing the laws.

_____

4. _____

_____

Students write routinely for a range of tasks, purposes, and audiences. Students practice various conventions of standard English.

Name _____

DIRECTIONS Use each word in a sentence.

disarray   haste

_____

_____

_____

_____

**Write in
Response to
Reading**

DIRECTIONS Write a paragraph that compares and contrasts the actions of First Woman and Coyote. Use specific details from the text to explain how each of their actions led to the outcome of the story.

_____

_____

_____

_____

_____

Students show contextual understanding of Benchmark Vocabulary. Students write routinely for a range of tasks, purposes, and audiences.

Name _____

DIRECTIONS Write a narrative paragraph that describes a tradition you practice in your family, at school, or within your culture or community. Use transitional words and phrases to clearly describe events in order.

_____

_____

_____

_____

Conventions

Compound Sentences Combine the sentence pair to form a compound sentence. Then write three of your own compound sentences about the theme of "How the Stars Fell into the Sky."

1. He crept closer. He still could not see her. (but)

_____

_____

2. _____

_____

3. _____

_____

4. _____

_____

Students write routinely for a range of tasks, purposes, and audiences. Students practice various conventions of standard English.

Name _____

DIRECTIONS Use each word in a sentence.

yarns   boastful   unsocialized   desolate

_____

_____

_____

_____

_____

_____

Write in Response to Reading

DIRECTIONS Reread pp. 51–54 of "Pecos Bill." Do you think Pecos Bill acts like a believable coyote? In what ways does he fall short of convincing you? Use details and examples from the text to support your answer.

_____

_____

_____

_____

Students show contextual understanding of Benchmark Vocabulary. Students write routinely for a range of tasks, purposes, and audiences.

Name _____

DIRECTIONS Write a descriptive paragraph about a character from another legend or fairy tale. Use vivid, descriptive language and specific sensory details to create imagery that will help your readers visualize what you are describing.

_____

_____

_____

_____

_____

Conventions

Complete Sentences Correct the run-on sentences. Then write two of your own sentences about Pecos Bill.

1. Pecos Bill was a cowboy, he spent time with coyotes.

_____

2. Even though he soon started dressing right, he never bothered to shave or comb his hair he'd just throw water on his face in the morning.

_____

_____

_____

3. _____

_____

4. _____

_____

Students write routinely for a range of tasks, purposes, and audiences. Students practice various conventions of standard English.

Name _____

DIRECTIONS Use each word in a sentence.

ignorant   dazed

_____

_____

_____

_____

Write in Response to Reading

DIRECTIONS Write a dialogue between yourself and Pecos Bill. Use language that reflects the way Pecos Bill speaks in the story. Revisit pp. 51–57 of "Pecos Bill" to help you.

_____

_____

_____

_____

_____

_____

_____

_____

Students show contextual understanding of Benchmark Vocabulary. Students write routinely for a range of tasks, purposes, and audiences.

Name _____

DIRECTIONS Using evidence from the text, answer the following questions about pp. 51–57 from "Pecos Bill."

1. What is an inference?

   _____

   _____

2. Reread the first paragraph on p. 54. What inference can you make about Pecos Bill's family?

   _____

   _____

   _____

3. Reread the dialogue on p. 55. What does this dialogue tell you about Pecos Bill?

   _____

   _____

   _____

4. How do the details on pp. 55–57 support the theme of this text?

   _____

   _____

   _____

Students analyze and respond to literary and informational text.

Name _____

DIRECTIONS Reread pp. 55–57 of "Pecos Bill." Write two paragraphs describing a **new** interaction between Pecos Bill and one of the cowpokes at the ranch. Your paragraphs should use dialogue and description to develop the characters. Remember to make your language similar to the language in the story.

_____

_____

_____

_____

_____

_____

_____

_____

_____

Conventions

Prepositional Phrases Circle the prepositional phrases in the sentences below.

1. Bill's folks loaded their fifteen kids and all their belongings into their covered wagon and started west.

2. The cowboys traveled many miles across the desert.

3. They had days of traveling ahead of them to reach the farm.

4. He would throw some water on his face every morning.

5. Bill tamed the snake with considerable skill.

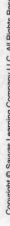

Students write routinely for a range of tasks, purposes, and audiences. Students practice various conventions of standard English.

Name _____

Suffixes -*ly*

Word Bank

cleverly	lonely	softly	widely
gloomily	recently	extremely	wisely
monthly	yearly	quickly	nervously
actually	hopefully	eagerly	

DIRECTIONS Complete each sentence with a list word.

1. When you have only one friend, sometimes you'll be _____.   1. _____

2. He solved the problem _____, using mathematics.   2. _____

3. He spends other people's money _____ but his own meagerly.   3. _____

4. While not _____ known, her music is very influential.   4. _____

5. Reporters write factually but _____ make mistakes.   5. _____

6. I love my great aunt dearly, but I only see her _____.   6. _____

7. I ran _____ to the store before it closed.   7. _____

8. Susan waited _____ to take her exam.   8. _____

9. Our new puppy _____ started to behave decently.   9. _____

10. The payment for his _____ magazine subscription was due.   10. _____

Antonyms Write the list word that has the opposite meaning of the underlined word.

11. He happily looked at the rain clouds above.   11. _____

12. The pianist played loudly, so as not to wake the neighbors.   12. _____

13. He foolishly did not talk about others.   13. _____

14. I find my hobby somewhat interesting.   14. _____

15. I doubtfully think I can go to the movies.   15. _____

Students apply grade-level phonics and word analysis skills.

Name _____

DIRECTIONS Use the word in a sentence.

drought

_____

_____

DIRECTIONS Reread pp. 58–61 of "Pecos Bill." How does the author's use of figurative language make the writing more vivid and exciting for the reader? Include examples of similes and metaphors from the text to support your answer.

_____

_____

_____

_____

_____

Students show contextual understanding of Benchmark Vocabulary. Students write routinely for a range of tasks, purposes, and audiences.

Name _____

DIRECTIONS Reread pp. 58–61 of "Pecos Bill." Write a paragraph about a character who could appear in a tall tale, such as "Pecos Bill." Use exaggeration and other types of figurative language to describe your character. In addition to exaggerated details, include at least one simile and one metaphor.

_____

_____

_____

_____

_____

Conventions

Relative Pronouns Circle the relative pronoun in the sentence below and underline the noun it describes. Then write three of your own sentences using relative pronouns.

1. There are many stories about Pecos Bill, who formed the Hell's Gate Gang!

2. _____

_____

3. _____

_____

4. _____

_____

Students write routinely for a range of tasks, purposes, and audiences. Students practice various conventions of standard English.

Name _____

DIRECTIONS Use each word in a sentence.

reverted   consequently   catastrophe

_____

_____

_____

_____

_____

Write in Response to Reading

DIRECTIONS Reread pp. 62–64 of "Pecos Bill." How does the author's word choice enhance the character descriptions in the story? Include examples from the text to support your answer.

_____

_____

_____

_____

_____

Students show contextual understanding of Benchmark Vocabulary. Students write routinely for a range of tasks, purposes, and audiences.

Name _____

DIRECTIONS Using evidence from the text, answer the following questions about pp. 62–64 of "Pecos Bill."

1. Why do authors of tall tales use nonliteral language, such as exaggeration?

   _____

   _____

2. List three examples of hyperbole, or extreme exaggeration, from the text.

   Example 1: _____

   _____

   Example 2: _____

   _____

   Example 3: _____

   _____

3. Choose one of the examples above, and explain how it helps the reader.

   _____

   _____

4. List two examples of figurative language.

   Example 1: _____

   Example 2: _____

5. Choose one of the examples and explain how it helps the reader.

   _____

   _____

Students analyze and respond to literary and informational text.

Name _____

DIRECTIONS Create a story sequence chart to help you plan a short narrative story about a day in the life of an adventurous child character. He or she might be a young detective, scientist, or athlete. Your sequence chart should describe your characters and setting, establish a situation, and plot events and a conclusion.

Conventions

Adverbs Circle the adverb in the sentence below, and underline the verb that it modifies. Then write three of your own sentences using adverbs.

1. When the Rio Grande dried up, they lassoed water from the Gulf of Mexico.

2. _____

_____

3. _____

_____

4. _____

_____

Students write routinely for a range of tasks, purposes, and audiences. Students practice various conventions of standard English.

Name _____

DIRECTIONS Use each word in a sentence.

regulations   superior   enduring   collapsed

_____

_____

_____

_____

_____

_____

DIRECTIONS Reread page 67 of "John Henry." Do you think the author used appropriate sensory details to describe the night John Henry was born? State your opinion and support it using evidence from the text.

_____

_____

_____

_____

Students show contextual understanding of Benchmark Vocabulary. Students write routinely for a range of tasks, purposes, and audiences.

The Strawberry: From Food to Fabric Softener

Do you like eating plump, juicy strawberries? When you think of strawberries, maybe you think of a fruity and crunchy topping on your cereal. Maybe you think of decadent dessert like strawberry shortcake. Have you ever thought of how else a strawberry might be used?

Many Native American cultures have shown how resourceful they could be. On the Great Plains, they hunted buffalo and used every part of it, from head to hoof, to meet their needs. Now their use of strawberries was a bit different. However, they did use them for much more than fuel for their bodies and fun for their taste buds. Native Americans used these succulent berries to make all sorts of things to meet their everyday needs.

Strawberries have a rich, deep red color. Native Americans figured out that they could use its color to produce red dye. Strawberry dye was a beautiful color and very long lasting. Native Americans colored cloth, animal skins, and even used it to paint their own skin.

Native Americans also made medicine from strawberry plants. Some turned the leaves into a tea, which helped people who suffered from stomach and kidney problems. Native Americans also made pastes out of the leaves and deer fat. These pastes healed burns and sores. Crushed berries could even be used to clean teeth! Some Native Americans even used strawberry plants to smell better. They made pads out of the leaves and put the pads inside their clothes to smell fresh. Think along the lines of deodorant, perfume, or even fabric softener!

Of course, Native Americans enjoyed eating strawberries just like we do today. They ate them fresh, used them to make jams, or dried them. Strawberries were not always available year-round. Drying them provided Native Americans with a supply to last all year.

Some Native American groups held a Strawberry Thanksgiving every June. They celebrated this red sweet delight by dancing, singing, and, of course, eating! They wanted to show their thanks for such a special fruit.

Students read text closely to determine what the text says.

Name _____

Gather Evidence Underline the uses for strawberries you find in the text. Briefly explain how you might group the uses.

_____

Gather Evidence: Extend Your Ideas Think of the uses for strawberry plants you identified. Choose three categories to describe them. Which uses would you put in each category?

_____

Ask Questions Circle something that was in the Native Americans' environment. Write two questions you want to research to learn more about how they used this in their lives.

_____

Ask Questions: Extend Your Ideas Look at the questions you wrote. Tell where you might look to find the answers to your questions.

_____

Make Your Case Draw a box around the words the author uses to describe strawberries. Choose three that you find most interesting. Briefly explain why you selected those words.

_____

Make Your Case: Extend Your Ideas Write the meanings of the three words you found most interesting. Then write two other words you would use to describe a strawberry.

_____

Prove It! Have students share their evidence with a classmate.

Students read text closely to determine what the text says.

Name _____

DIRECTIONS Prewrite and plan for a draft of the first paragraph of your narrative about a day in the life of a child. Your paragraph should focus on describing the setting and introducing the main character. Revisit "Pecos Bill" or "John Henry" to help you.

_____

_____

_____

_____

_____

Conventions

Progressive Verb Tenses Rewrite the sentence using the simple past tense of each underlined verb. Then write three of your own sentences using progressive verb tenses.

1. Pecos Bill settles down with the Hell's Gate Gang, uses New Mexico as a corral, and invents tarantulas.

_____

_____

2. _____

_____

3. _____

_____

4. _____

_____

Students write routinely for a range of tasks, purposes, and audiences. Students practice various conventions of standard English.

Name _____

DIRECTIONS Use the word in a sentence.

dignity

_____

_____

**Write in
Response to
Reading**

DIRECTIONS Reread p. 69 of "John Henry." What are some of the ways that John Henry shows what is most important to him? Use details and examples from the text to support your answer.

_____

_____

_____

_____

_____

Students show contextual understanding
of Benchmark Vocabulary. Students write
routinely for a range of tasks, purposes, and
audiences.

DIRECTIONS Using evidence from the text, answer the following questions about pp. 65–69 from "John Henry."

1. What sentence shows the railroad bosses' motivation to try to hire John Henry?

   _____

   _____

2. What line(s) of dialogue shows why John Henry helped the steel drivers keep their jobs by doing their work after they collapsed?

   _____

   _____

   _____

3. What was John Henry's boss' motivation for wanting John Henry to compete against the steam drill?

   _____

   _____

4. What was Lucy's motivation for not wanting John Henry to compete against the steam drill?

   _____

   _____

5. What does Lucy's motivation tell you about her character? Use evidence from the text to support your answer.

   _____

   _____

Students analyze and respond to literary and informational text.

Name _____

DIRECTIONS Write one or two paragraphs for the narrative you began in Lesson 13. Focus on adding dialogue and descriptions to develop the personalities and experiences of your characters. Use concrete words and sensory details, and punctuate your dialogue correctly.

_____

_____

_____

_____

_____

Conventions

Frequently Confused Words Circle the correct word in the first sentence. Then write three of your own sentences using the frequently confused words below.

heal heel   weight wait   their there

1. Bill's horse stepped in a whole/ hole and broke its ankle.

2. _____

_____

3. _____

_____

4. _____

_____

Students write routinely for a range of tasks, purposes, and audiences. Students practice various conventions of standard English.

Name _____

DIRECTIONS Use each word in a sentence.

contestants billowed

_____

_____

_____

_____

Write in Response to Reading

DIRECTIONS Reread pp. 70–71 of "John Henry." What do you think John Henry means to the people around him, including his wife, boss, and coworkers? Use details from the text to support your answer.

_____

_____

_____

_____

Students show contextual understanding of Benchmark Vocabulary. Students write routinely for a range of tasks, purposes, and audiences.

Name _____

DIRECTIONS Revise the narrative you began in Lesson 13 to make the sequence of events clearer. Add transitional words and phrases that clearly show the order and timing of events. Then rearrange, add, or delete information as necessary.

_____

_____

_____

_____

_____

_____

_____

_____

_____

_____

Conventions

Progressive Verb Tenses Underline the progressive verb tenses in the sentences below.

1. Then John Henry grabbed another hammer and was working with a hammer in each hand.

2. The men will be working on a new stretch of the railroad.

3. Many of the steel drivers are hoping for a bright future.

4. The owner of these new machines will be holding a demonstration tomorrow.

Students write routinely for a range of tasks, purposes, and audiences. Students practice various conventions of standard English.

Name _____

Unknown Words

Word Bank

omitted	verbose	articulate	subside
terse	friable	extravagant	dainty

DIRECTIONS Use context clues to determine the meaning of the underlined words in the following sentences.

I see that you left out information in your application. Why was it <u>omitted</u>?

1. _____

The speaker was very <u>articulate</u>. Did you know that she could speak so well?

2. _____

Her new puppy was quite <u>dainty</u>. Its paws were tiny and delicate.

3. _____

We attended an <u>extravagant</u> party. There was endless food, and a full orchestra.

4. _____

DIRECTIONS Write the meaning of the underlined words.

Eventually the waves began to <u>subside</u>, and everything was calm again.

5. _____

He used very few words when he spoke. I never realized he was so <u>terse</u>.

6. _____

The fourth grader was <u>verbose</u>, using too many challenging words in his writing.

7. _____

I ate a <u>friable</u> pastry and got crumbs and flakes all over my new shirt.

8. _____

Students apply grade-level phonics and word analysis skills.

Name _____

DIRECTIONS Use each word in a sentence.

clutched   flagged

_____

_____

_____

_____

_____

**Write in
Response to
Reading**

DIRECTIONS Reread pp. 71–73 of "John Henry." How do John Henry's physical qualities and actions make him a suitable main character for a tall tale? Use evidence from the text to support your answer.

_____

_____

_____

_____

_____

Students show contextual understanding of Benchmark Vocabulary. Students write routinely for a range of tasks, purposes, and audiences.

Name _____

DIRECTIONS Write a strong conclusion to your narrative about the life of an adventurous child. Determine how you want the main problem or conflict to end. Then consider what lessons the main character has learned, or what values the story teaches. Remember that your conclusion should wrap up loose ends and leave a strong impression on your reader.

_____

_____

_____

_____

_____

Conventions

Punctuate Direct Speech and Quotations Correctly punctuate the following dialogue. Then write your own dialogue using correct punctuation.

1. Aw, I don't know about that, said the railroad boss, rubbing his grizzly jaw. I got the best steel driver in the country. His name is John Henry, and he can beat two dozen men working together.

2. No, sirree! said Jimmy, John Henry's oldest friend. Before that drill wins, he'll make the mountain fall!

3. _____

_____

_____

Students write routinely for a range of tasks, purposes, and audiences. Students practice various conventions of standard English.

Name _____

DIRECTIONS Use each word in a sentence.

disarray   catastrophe   enduring   preserve

_____

_____

_____

_____

_____

**Write in
Response to
Reading**

DIRECTIONS Think about the behavior of coyotes in "Pecos Bill" and "How the Stars Fell into the Sky." How do their actions make you feel about them? Include examples from both texts to support your answer.

_____

_____

_____

_____

_____

_____

_____

Students show contextual understanding of Benchmark Vocabulary. Students write routinely for a range of tasks, purposes, and audiences.

Name _____

DIRECTIONS Using evidence from both texts, answer the following questions about "Pecos Bill" and "John Henry."

1. How are the author's language choices similar in "Pecos Bill" and "John Henry"?

   _____

   _____

2. Give an example from each text of similar language choices.

   _____

   _____

   _____

3. Why do you think the texts have similar language choices?

   _____

   _____

4. How are the author's language choices different in "Pecos Bill" and in "John Henry"? Give examples.

   _____

   _____

5. What other comparisons can you make about the language choices in the two texts?

   _____

   _____

Students analyze and respond to literary and informational text.

Name _____

DIRECTIONS Edit and proofread your narrative about a day in the life of an adventurous child. Check that you have used transitional words and an event sequence that makes sense. Remember to include dialogue and descriptive details that clearly relate to your character's experiences. Then, check your grammar, spelling, punctuation, and sentence structure.

_____

_____

_____

_____

_____

Using Dictionaries Look up each word in bold in the dictionary. Write the definition that matches the use of each word. Then choose a word from the text that you don't know and look it up in the dictionary. Write the definition.

1. He saw men robbed of their **dignity** and robbed of their families.

_____

2. Bill **sidled** up to their campfire.

_____

3. Most men would have **smothered** in the dank heat of that tunnel.

_____

4. _____

Name _____

DIRECTIONS Use each word in a sentence.

enormous   haste   reverted   dignity

_____

_____

_____

_____

Write in Response to Reading

DIRECTIONS Write a paragraph in which you compare the effects of language choices in two of the four texts. You may use examples from *Why the Sea Is Salty,* "How the Stars Fell into the Sky," "Pecos Bill," or "John Henry."

_____

_____

_____

_____

_____

_____

_____

_____

_____

Students show contextual understanding of Benchmark Vocabulary. Students write routinely for a range of tasks, purposes, and audiences.

Name _____

DIRECTIONS Publish and present your narrative about a day in the life of an adventurous child. Remember to include at least one visual to support your writing. Practice presenting your published writing with clarity and confidence. Then present your narrative to the class.

_____

_____

_____

_____

Conventions

Capitalize Correctly Rewrite each sentence below as if it were the title of a book. Remember to use correct capitalization.

1. steel drivers of the allegheny mountains

_____

2. pecos bill meets the hell's gate gang

_____

3. john henry and the steam drill

_____

4. bill and sue fall in love and get married

_____

Students write routinely for a range of tasks, purposes, and audiences. Students practice various conventions of standard English.

Words from Latin

Word Bank

spectacle	prospect	import	species
population	portable	transport	export
expect	passport	opportunity	inspector
respect	aspect	speculate	

Words in Context Write a list word to complete each sentence.

1. I don't agree with one ____of your argument.   1. _____

2. She has a great ____to travel to China.   2. _____

3. They studied many different ____of frogs.   3. _____

4. We ____tractors to Thailand.   4. _____

5. I ____to graduate in June 2024.   5. _____

6. A good scientist would ____about what caused this.   6. _____

7. I ____ the great job you've done this year!   7. _____

8. We ____toys from South America.   8. _____

9. The girls bought a ____stove for their camping trip.   9. _____

10. The local ____was very kind to us during our visit.   10. _____

11. Jumbo jets ____goods across the ocean.   11. _____

12. You must have a ____to visit a foreign country.   12. _____

13. The ____ of having to rebuild after the storm is difficult.   13. _____

14. The restaurant owner was waiting for the food ____.   14. _____

15. It was a ____ with flashing lights and fireworks.   15. _____

Students apply grade-level phonics and word analysis skills.

Name _____

DIRECTIONS Use each word in a sentence.

quest   sacred   warrior   triumph

_____

_____

_____

_____

_____

Write in Response to Reading

DIRECTIONS Reread pp. 4–7 of *The Longest Night*. What is your opinion of Wind Runner? What kind of person do you think he is? Use evidence from the text to support your answer.

_____

_____

_____

_____

_____

Students show contextual understanding of Benchmark Vocabulary. Students write routinely for a range of tasks, purposes, and audiences.

Name _____

DIRECTIONS Write an opinion paragraph explaining how Wind Runner felt about his Vision Quest. Use evidence and details from the text to support your opinion.

_____

_____

_____

_____

_____

Conventions

Capitalize Titles Correctly Rewrite the titles below correctly. Then write the titles of three of your favorite books, movies, or songs using correct capitalization.

1. the Wizard Of oz

_____

2. Harry Potter And The Sorcerer's Stone

_____

3. _____

4. _____

5. _____

Students write routinely for a range of tasks, purposes, and audiences. Students practice various conventions of standard English.

Name _____

Greek Roots

Word Groups Write the list word that best fits into each group.

1. topic sentence, supporting sentence, ____

1. _____

2. life story, nonfiction, ____

2. _____

3. line, fence, __

3. _____

4. film, camera, ____

4. _____

5. dance, practice, ____

5. _____

6. voice, record, ____

6. _____

7. instrument, metal, ____

7. _____

8. signature, celebrity, ____

8. _____

9. universe, lens, ____

9. _____

10. weather, air pressure, ____

10. _____

telephone

biography

telescope

photograph

autograph

perimeter

barometer

microphone

choreography

telegraph

thermos

paragraph

phonics

symphony

saxophone

Word Groups Write the list word that best completes each sentence.

11. I waited for his ____ call.

11. _____

12. My mom uses a ____ to keep her coffee warm.

12. _____

13. We heard such beautiful music at the ____last night.

13. _____

14. Beginning readers learn ____ to help them sound out new words.

14. _____

15. Morse code, a series of dots and dashes, was sent by ____.

15. _____

Students apply grade-level phonics and word analysis skills.

Name _____

DIRECTIONS Use each word in a sentence.

chanted   shallow   raked

_____

_____

_____

_____

_____

Write in Response to Reading

DIRECTIONS Reread pp. 10–11 of *The Longest Night*. What does Many Horses say that makes Wind Runner feel uncomfortable? Use evidence and details from the text to support your answer.

_____

_____

_____

_____

Students show contextual understanding of Benchmark Vocabulary. Students write routinely for a range of tasks, purposes, and audiences.

Name _____

DIRECTIONS Using evidence from the text, answer the following questions about pp. 8–12 from *The Longest Night*.

1. Reread the third paragraph on p. 8. What does the word *waft* mean?

_____

_____

2. What clues can you use to help you figure out the meaning of *waft?*

_____

_____

3. Reread the second paragraph on p. 10. Why does Wind Runner use the word *ancient* to describe the elder?

_____

_____

_____

4. How do you know?

_____

_____

_____

5. Reread the first paragraph on p. 11. What word could the author have used instead of *shame?*

_____

_____

Students analyze and respond to literary and informational text.

Name _____

DIRECTIONS Reread pp. 8–12 of *The Longest Night*. Write an opinion paragraph describing whether or not you think Wind Runner is a brave character. Use evidence from the text to support your answer.

_____

_____

_____

_____

_____

Conventions

Correct Capitalization Write three sentences that contain the names of individual people, places, and things. Remember to use correct capitalization.

1. _____

_____

2. _____

_____

3. _____

_____

Students write routinely for a range of tasks, purposes, and audiences. Students practice various conventions of standard English.

Name _____

DIRECTIONS Use each word in a sentence.

endured   ritual   retrieved   tribute

_____

_____

_____

_____

_____

Write in Response to Reading

DIRECTIONS Reread pp. 16–19 of *The Longest Night*. Why does Wind Runner decide to climb all the way to the top of the mountain instead of stopping? Use details from the text to support your answer.

_____

_____

_____

_____

_____

Students show contextual understanding of Benchmark Vocabulary. Students write routinely for a range of tasks, purposes, and audiences.

Learning a New Language

There was a buzz in the classroom. Mrs. Taylor announced that a new student was joining the class soon, and the student was coming from Mexico.

After the announcement, Mrs. Taylor asked everyone to quiet down. "I know you're excited about our new student," she said, "but I have some other good news too."

"Our principal, Mrs. Littlefield, and I have decided that it'd be helpful for us to learn some Spanish. That'll help us communicate better with Alita. She can learn English while we learn Spanish," Mrs. Taylor explained.

Mrs. Taylor's class broke out in cheers of excitement. "I know some Spanish already," informed Kelly. "My grandparents speak Spanish."

"Great!" Mrs. Taylor responded. "You can help us learn Spanish too. We have a guest coming today who's a Spanish tutor. He's going to teach us some Spanish language basics."

Just then a man walked in and introduced himself. "Hello, or *hola!* I'm Señor Alvarez, and I'll be working with you over the next few weeks. Before you know it, you'll be able to have a simple conversation with Alita."

Señor Alvarez began the first lesson. "There are a few tips that I'd like to share with you. Remember these, and you'll have an easier time learning a new language.

"First, you'll want to spend as much time as you can listening to the language, so I'll leave some Spanish language CDs for you. Listen to these and practice saying the words with the speaker.

"The second tip is to spend time every day studying. I'll be here twice a week, and when I'm not here, work together in a small group and practice what you have learned.

"The third, and maybe the most important tip, is not to worry about making mistakes. Sometimes you make mistakes even when you're speaking English, so don't worry about making mistakes when you're trying to learn how to speak Spanish. Don't be afraid to ask me or Alita, when she arrives, how to say or pronounce something."

Señor Alvarez then taught the class how to say a few words and phrases in Spanish. After the tutoring session ended, many students were eager to practice. The students were excited about being able to greet Alita in Spanish when she arrived!

Students read text closely to determine what the text says.

Name _____

Gather Evidence Circle the new language that Mrs. Taylor wants her class to learn. Write evidence from the story to explain why she thinks learning this new language will be helpful for her students.

_____

_____

Gather Evidence: Extend Your Ideas Write additional reasons for learning a new language.

_____

_____

Ask Questions Draw a box around the name of the country Alita comes from. Write several questions that you might ask Alita about her home and life in another country.

_____

_____

Ask Questions: Extend Your Ideas Write three questions you would like to learn to ask, in Spanish, of a new student in your school.

_____

_____

Make Your Case Underline the names of people who speak in the story. How do the words spoken by the characters help us to learn about them? Use examples from the story and explain what they tell about the characters.

_____

_____

Make Your Case: Extend Your Ideas Briefly explain why communication is important to people across the world.

_____

_____

Students read text closely to determine what the text says.

Lesson 3

Name _____

Writing

DIRECTIONS Write two or three paragraphs on a separate sheet of paper about whether or not you think Wind Runner will successfully complete his Vision Quest. Base your response on pp. 13–23 of *The Longest Night.* Remember to group related information into paragraphs. Use details from the text to support your answer.

Conventions

Use Capitalization Correctly Write two sentences about the Shaman and Wind Runner's Vision Quest, using capitalization like the author does. Then write one sentence, unrelated to the text, in which *shaman* and *vision quest* aren't capitalized.

1. _____

   _____

2. _____

   _____

3. _____

   _____

Students write routinely for a range of tasks, purposes, and audiences. Students practice various conventions of standard English.

Name _____

DIRECTIONS Use each word in a sentence.

ancestors   recoiled   serpent   obstacle

_____

_____

_____

_____

_____

_____

_____

Write in Response to Reading

DIRECTIONS Reread pp. 27–28 of *The Longest Night*. Why does the snake go around the dog? What details does the author provide that help you visualize the scene? Use evidence from the text to support your answer.

_____

_____

_____

_____

Students show contextual understanding of Benchmark Vocabulary. Students write routinely for a range of tasks, purposes, and audiences.

Name _____

DIRECTIONS Reread pp. 24–29 of *The Longest Night.* Pay close attention to how Wind Runner treats the dog. Then write an opinion paragraph about whether or not you think Wind Runner had good reasons to treat the dog the way he did. Use evidence and details from the text to support your answer.

_____

_____

_____

_____

_____

Conventions

Understand Pronouns Circle the pronoun and underline the noun it replaces. Then write two sentences of your own using pronouns.

1. Sheila had no interest in the television show, so she turned it off.

2. Wind Runner watched quietly as the grizzly bear licked its lips and growled.

3. The Worthless One sat outside the circle and howled. Its tail angled toward the sky.

4. _____

_____

5. _____

_____

Students write routinely for a range of tasks, purposes, and audiences. Students practice various conventions of standard English.

Lesson 5

Benchmark Vocabulary

Name _____

DIRECTIONS Use each word in a sentence.

vigorously   futile   prey   predators

_____

_____

_____

_____

_____

_____

_____

Write in Response to Reading

DIRECTIONS Reread pp. 30–37 of *The Longest Night*. What is Wind Runner's opinion of The Worthless One? Do you think his opinion is beginning to change? Use details from the text to support your answer.

_____

_____

_____

_____

_____

_____

_____

Students show contextual understanding of Benchmark Vocabulary. Students write routinely for a range of tasks, purposes, and audiences.

Name _____

DIRECTIONS Using evidence from the text, answer the following questions about pp. 30–37 from *The Longest Night*.

1. Reread p. 32. What is one example of figurative language on this page?

   _____

   _____

2. Reread p. 35. What is one example of hyperbole on this page?

   _____

   _____

3. Select one of the examples you found and rewrite it using your own words. Which do you prefer—the author's use of language or your own?

   _____

   _____

   _____

4. Write a paragraph about whether or not you think figurative language enhances a text. Use evidence and details from the text to support your answer.

   _____

   _____

   _____

   _____

Students analyze and respond to literary and informational text.

Lesson 5

Name _____

Writing

DIRECTIONS Reread the second paragraph on p. 35 of *The Longest Night*. Write an opinion paragraph about whether or not Wind Runner deserves a Spirit Helper. Use information from the entire chapter to support your opinion. Support your opinion by paraphrasing and quoting accurately from the text.

_____

_____

_____

_____

_____

Conventions

Punctuate Dialogue Write your own dialogue using correct punctuation.

_____

_____

_____

_____

_____

_____

_____

_____

_____

Students write routinely for a range of tasks, purposes, and audiences. Students practice various conventions of standard English.

Related Words

Words in Context Write two related list words to complete each sentence.

It would **(1)** _____ me greatly if you were nicer

and more **(2)** _____ to our neighbors.

My friend says being a **(3)** _____ means she

and her two look-alike sisters have **(4)** _____

the fun.

The company rushed to get the new **(5)** _____

into **(6)** _____ in time for the holiday sales.

Don't **(7)** _____ on me with your bad

(8) _____!

A **(9)** _____ is a basic unit of length in the

(10) _____ system.

The wound will **(11)** _____, and then you will be

the picture of perfect **(12)** _____.

At family gatherings, there's always at least one

(13) _____ who likes to **(14)** _____ old

family stories.

Mozart had the ability to **(15)** _____ a lengthy

musical **(16)** _____ in a short time.

Word Bank

please
pleasant
breath
breathe
product
production
heal
health
triple
triplet
relate
relative
meter
metric
compose
composition

Students apply grade-level phonics and word analysis skills.

DIRECTIONS Use each word in a sentence.

lumbered   gazed   foraged   arrogant

_____

_____

_____

_____

_____

_____

_____

Write in Response to Reading

DIRECTIONS Reread pp. 38–42 of *The Longest Night*. What challenges does Wind Runner face on these pages? How does he deal with those challenges? Use evidence from the text to support your answer.

_____

_____

_____

_____

_____

Students show contextual understanding of Benchmark Vocabulary. Students write routinely for a range of tasks, purposes, and audiences.

Name _____

DIRECTIONS Write a paragraph about whether or not Wind Runner would have been successful without the aid of a Spirit Helper. Use evidence from the text to support your answer.

_____

_____

_____

_____

_____

_____

_____

_____

Conventions

Adjectives Identify the adjectives as positive, comparative, or superlative.

1. Brave _____

2. Coldest _____

3. Hardest _____

4. Warmer _____

5. Heavy _____

Students write routinely for a range of tasks, purposes, and audiences. Students practice various conventions of standard English.

Name _____

DIRECTIONS Use each word in a sentence.

abundance   possessions   contact   heritage

_____

_____

_____

_____

_____

_____

_____

Write in Response to Reading

DIRECTIONS Reread pp. 106–107 of "Northwest Coast Peoples." What was village life like for peoples of the Northwest Coast? Use evidence from the text to support your answer.

_____

_____

_____

_____

_____

Students show contextual understanding of Benchmark Vocabulary. Students write routinely for a range of tasks, purposes, and audiences.

Name _____

DIRECTIONS Using evidence from the text, answer the following questions about pp. 103–111 of "Northwest Coast Peoples."

1. Reread the first paragraph on p. 104. What is the main idea of this paragraph?

   _____

   _____

2. What details support the main idea?

   _____

   _____

3. Reread the first paragraph on p. 110. What is the main idea of this paragraph?

   _____

   _____

4. What details support the main idea?

   _____

   _____

5. Reread p. 111. What are some of the ways a *totem pole* was used?

   _____

   _____

   _____

Students analyze and respond to literary and informational text.

Lesson 7

Name _____

Writing

DIRECTIONS Revisit pp. 104–111 of "Northwest Coast Peoples." Write an opinion about which visual you think best enhances the information in this section. Use evidence from the text to support your answer.

_____

_____

_____

_____

_____

Conventions

Punctuate Direct Quotations Rewrite the sentences below using correct punctuation.

1. Bill said, I am going to the zoo.

_____

2. It's almost time for my Vision Quest," said Wind Runner.

_____

3. Children living in Northwest Coast villages have an active life, said Mrs. Monroe.

_____

_____

4. We're going to study village life now," our teacher said, so let's pay close attention to this presentation.

_____

_____

Students write routinely for a range of tasks, purposes, and audiences. Students practice various conventions of standard English.

Name _____

DIRECTIONS Use each word in a sentence.

significant   activists   traditional

_____

_____

_____

_____

_____

Write in Response to Reading

DIRECTIONS Reread pp. 114–115 of "Northwest Coast Peoples."
What happened when Russian, Spanish, and British ships began sailing
to the Northwest Coast? Were these interactions positive or negative? Use
evidence from the text to support your answer.

_____

_____

_____

_____

_____

_____

_____

Students show contextual understanding
of Benchmark Vocabulary. Students write
routinely for a range of tasks, purposes,
and audiences.

DIRECTIONS Plan and prewrite for a piece that supports your opinion about which text more accurately describes Native American culture. You should plan for a text in which you state an opinion and support it with reasons. Use a graphic organizer to gather any text evidence you plan to use.

_____

_____

_____

_____

_____

Conventions

Punctuating Dialogue Rewrite the dialogue correctly. Then write your own dialogue between two or more Northwest Coast Native Americans on the lines below.

1. our community hasn't been the same since the Russians arrived. The Elder replied that is true.

   _____

   _____

2. _____

   _____

   _____

   _____

   _____

Students write routinely for a range of tasks, purposes, and audiences. Students practice various conventions of standard English.

Name _____

DIRECTIONS Use each word in a sentence.

quest   ancestors   heritage   traditional

_____

_____

_____

_____

_____

_____

_____

**Write in
Response to
Reading**

DIRECTIONS Revisit *The Longest Night* and "Northwest Coast
Peoples." How are these texts alike? How are they different? Use evidence
from both texts to support your answer.

_____

_____

_____

_____

Students show contextual understanding
of Benchmark Vocabulary. Students write
routinely for a range of tasks, purposes,
and audiences.

Name _____

DIRECTIONS Write several paragraphs about which text you think more accurately describes Native American culture. Use your planning and prewriting from Lesson 8 to help you. Remember to state your opinion clearly, group related information into paragraphs, and support your opinion with facts and details from the text.

_____

_____

_____

_____

_____

_____

_____

_____

Conventions

Complete Sentences Write your own sentences on the lines below. Use coordinating conjunctions.

1. _____

_____

2. _____

_____

3. _____

_____

Students write routinely for a range of tasks, purposes, and audiences. Students practice various conventions of standard English.

Name _____

DIRECTIONS Use each word in a sentence.

alliance   legend   festivals

_____

_____

_____

_____

_____

_____

**Write in
Response to
Reading**

DIRECTIONS Reread pp. 6–7 of *Three Native Nations: Of the
Woodlands, Plains, and Desert*. Write several sentences about the different
roles of men and women in the Haudenosaunee nation. Use evidence from
the text to support your answer.

_____

_____

_____

_____

_____

Students show contextual understanding
of Benchmark Vocabulary. Students write
routinely for a range of tasks, purposes,
and audiences.

Name _____

DIRECTIONS Using evidence from the text, answer the following questions about pp. 4–9 of *Three Native Nations: Of the Woodlands, Plains, and Desert.*

1. Reread the first paragraph on p. 6. What is the main idea of this paragraph?

   _____

   _____

2. What details support the main idea?

   _____

   _____

3. Reread pp. 8–9. What do you learn about the roles of women in society on these pages?

   _____

   _____

4. What is a *longhouse*? How do you know?

   _____

   _____

5. What is an *ohwachira*? How do you know?

   _____

   _____

Students analyze and respond to literary and informational text.

Name _____

DIRECTIONS Write a brief summary of pp. 4–9 of *Three Native Nations: Of the Woodlands, Plains, and Desert.* Your summary should include your opinion about why you think women of the *ohwachira* chose the clan leaders. Use evidence from the text to support your opinion.

_____

_____

_____

_____

_____

Conventions

Producing Compound Sentences Use information from *Three Native Nations: Of the Woodlands, Plains, and Desert* to write three compound sentences.

1. _____

_____

_____

2. _____

_____

_____

3. _____

_____

_____

Students write routinely for a range of tasks, purposes, and audiences. Students practice various conventions of standard English.

Latin Roots *struct, scrib, scrip*

Word Bank

description	scribe	scribbling	instrument	destruct
manuscript	suspect	subscription	instructions	circumscribe
construct	inscription	obstruct	prescribes	scribble

Words in Context Write the list words that complete each sentence.

She paged through the mystery (1) _____ and became

convinced that the main (2) _____ was guilty.

If your doctor (3) _____ you some medication, then be sure

to follow her (4) _____.

The article describes an antique stringed (5) _____ with an

(6) _____ from the late king on it.

I didn't mean to (7) _____ the class with my ferocious

(8) _____. I just love drawing.

The (9) _____ of the baseball game in the newspaper

was boring. However, the food section included clear

(10) _____ about making a cake from scratch!

Word Definitions Write the list word that has the same meaning.

11. purchase a series of things   11. _____

12. a copier of manuscripts   12. _____

13. write carelessly   13. _____

14. to destroy or damage   14. _____

15. to restrict something   15. _____

Students apply grade-level phonics and word
analysis skills.

Name _____

DIRECTIONS Use each word in a sentence.

clan   descendants   reservation

_____

_____

_____

_____

_____

**Write in
Response to
Reading**

DIRECTIONS Reread pp. 12–15 of *Three Native Nations: Of the
Woodlands, Plains, and Desert.* What changes did the Haudenosaunee
experience over time? Use details from the text to support your answer.

_____

_____

_____

_____

Students show contextual understanding
of Benchmark Vocabulary. Students write
routinely for a range of tasks, purposes,
and audiences.

DIRECTIONS Write two paragraphs in which you state an opinion about what daily life would be like living in a longhouse. State your opinion clearly and concisely. Remember to support your opinion using text evidence such as quotations, paraphrases, or description of visuals.

_____

_____

_____

_____

_____

_____

_____

Conventions

Complete Sentences Circle the main clause and underline the extra clause in the sentences below. Then write two of your own complete sentences.

1. Since there were no schools, boys and girls learned by following around their fathers or mothers.

2. Because the French and British were at war, members of the Iroquois League took sides in the conflict to protect their families.

3. _____

_____

4. _____

_____

Students write routinely for a range of tasks, purposes, and audiences. Students practice various conventions of standard English.

Name _____

DIRECTIONS Use each word in a sentence.

revered   nourished   continent

_____

_____

_____

_____

_____

**Write in
Response to
Reading**

DIRECTIONS Reread the third paragraph on p. 20 of *Three Native Nations: Of the Woodlands, Plains, and Desert.* What is the main idea of this paragraph? How do you know? Use details from the text to support your answer.

_____

_____

_____

_____

Students show contextual understanding of Benchmark Vocabulary. Students write routinely for a range of tasks, purposes, and audiences.

Name _____

DIRECTIONS Using evidence from the text, answer the following questions about pp. 18–25 of *Three Native Nations: Of the Woodlands, Plains, and Desert*.

1. Reread pp. 22-23. What is the main idea of this section?

_____

2. What details support the main idea?

_____

_____

3. Write a paragraph in which you summarize pp. 22–23. Use the main idea and details above to help you summarize the text.

_____

_____

_____

_____

_____

4. Reread p. 24. Identify the main idea and details. Then summarize the section on the lines below.

_____

_____

_____

_____

Students analyze and respond to literary and informational text.

Name _____

DIRECTIONS Plan and prewrite for a piece in which you will compare two sections of *Three Native Nations: Of the Woodlands, Plains, and Desert,* telling which one you find more interesting and compelling. Use a graphic organizer to gather text evidence that you plan to use.

_____

_____

_____

_____

_____

_____

_____

Conventions

Commas and Coordinating Conjunctions Circle the coordinating conjunction. Underline the word that a comma should follow. Then write your own compound sentences using commas and coordinating conjunctions.

1. The swamp grass rippled and dogs napped in the sun.

2. Wind Runner could be brave or he could falter in his quest.

3. _____

_____

4. _____

_____

Students write routinely for a range of tasks, purposes, and audiences. Students practice various conventions of standard English.

Name _____

DIRECTIONS Use each word in a sentence.

quill   social   custom

_____

_____

_____

_____

Write in Response to Reading

DIRECTIONS Reread pp. 28–29 of *Three Native Nations: Of the Woodlands, Plains, and Desert.* How did the arrival of horses change daily life for the Lakota? Use details from the text to support your answer.

_____

_____

_____

_____

_____

Students show contextual understanding of Benchmark Vocabulary. Students write routinely for a range of tasks, purposes, and audiences.

Name _____

American Melting Pot?

How would you feel if your family decided to move to China, Egypt, or Spain? You might not speak the language. The food could be different. You would face a very different culture. Would you expect teachers in your new school to speak English? Or would you need to learn the language and customs as fast as possible?

Except for Native Americans, every person living in the United States can trace his or her ancestry back to a different country. About 12.5% of Americans today were born in other countries. Some people think that those who come here should learn the customs and language of this country. In the early twentieth century, Israel Zangwill wrote a play called *The Melting Pot.* In it, he said America is like a melting pot. He suggested that immigrants are blended together and transformed into "Americans."

Many have disagreed with that view. Former New York Representative Shirley Chisholm said, "We are nobody's melting pot!" She said, "We are a beautiful, giant salad bowl." She thought that the character and strength of America lies in the contributions of its people. The people are from many different racial, ethnic, and cultural groups. In the "salad bowl" idea, each ingredient (people of a different culture) keeps its own identity.

So, how can a person stay true to his or her heritage and still be "American"? How can and should schools promote the roles of various racial, ethnic, and cultural groups in society? Should the school cafeteria take into account religious and cultural food restrictions? Should the dress code allow for cultural differences? Should teachers be required to teach in several languages?

Educators, politicians, parents, and students debate these questions. Fear and prejudice and an "us versus them" mentality occur when different groups don't understand one another. Schools might be an ideal place to get to know people from other cultures. What do you think? How should schools encourage students to focus on what people have in common while still valuing and respecting their differences?

Students read text closely to determine what the text says.

Name _____

Gather Evidence In the text, circle what it means to say America is a "melting pot." Underline what it means to say America is a "salad bowl." Briefly explain what the text says about each.

_____

_____

Gather Evidence: Extend Your Ideas Focusing on the parts of the text you identified, explain in your own words what it means to say American society is a "salad bowl" or a "melting pot."

_____

_____

Ask Questions Draw a box around three things in the text that you would like to research about how U.S. schools are adapting to ethnic, cultural, and religious differences among students. Write three questions you might ask.

_____

_____

Ask Questions: Extend Your Ideas Write additional questions you could ask about how U.S. schools are adapting.

_____

_____

Make Your Case Put a box around three challenging words from the text. List them. Using resources to help define each word, which definition of each word is the best fit for the context of this text?

_____

_____

Make Your Case: Extend Your Ideas Choose another challenging word from the text, and give the definition that best fits the context of the text.

_____

_____

Students read text closely to determine what the text says.

Name _____

DIRECTIONS Craft an introductory paragraph for the opinion essay you planned in Lesson 12. Remember to use a strategy that will motivate the reader to learn more about the opinion. Revisit the text and your notes to help you.

_____

_____

_____

_____

_____

_____

Conventions

Compound Sentences Write three of your own compound sentences.

1. _____

_____

2. _____

_____

3. _____

_____

Students write routinely for a range of tasks, purposes, and audiences. Students practice various conventions of standard English.

Name _____

DIRECTIONS Use each word in a sentence.

irrigation   fashion

_____

_____

_____

_____

> **Write in Response to Reading**

DIRECTIONS Reread pp. 36–37 of *Three Native Nations: Of the Woodlands, Plains, and Desert.* What is the main idea of this section? What details support this main idea? Use details from the text to support your answer.

_____

_____

_____

_____

_____

Students show contextual understanding of Benchmark Vocabulary. Students write routinely for a range of tasks, purposes, and audiences.

Name _____

DIRECTIONS Reread pp. 32–39 of *Three Native Nations: Of the Woodlands, Plains, and Desert,* paying close attention to the visuals. Then write a paragraph giving your opinion about which of the visuals best supports the text. Identify the pages on which the visual and the text appear. Explain how the visual relates to the text and why you think it is the best choice. Use details from the text to support your opinion.

_____

_____

_____

_____

_____

_____

_____

Conventions

Progressive Verb Tenses Circle the progressive verb tense in the following sentences. Then write two of your own sentences using progressive verb tenses.

1. The women are grilling meat next to the longhouse.

2. The Pueblo farmers will be using irrigation to keep their crops moist.

3. _____

_____

4. _____

_____

Students write routinely for a range of tasks, purposes, and audiences. Students practice various conventions of standard English.

Name _____

DIRECTIONS Use the word in a sentence.

dominated

_____

_____

_____

Write in Response to Reading

DIRECTIONS Reread pp. 40–43 of *Three Native Nations: Of the Woodlands, Plains, and Desert*. What did boys and girls learn to do? How is a *kiva* different from an *adobe* home? Use evidence from the text to support your answer.

_____

_____

_____

_____

_____

_____

_____

_____

Students show contextual understanding of Benchmark Vocabulary. Students write routinely for a range of tasks, purposes, and audiences.

DIRECTIONS Using evidence from the text, answer the following questions about pp. 40–46 of *Three Native Nations: Of the Woodlands, Plains, and Desert.*

1. Reread pp. 40–41. Do boys and girls learn the same skills?

_____

_____

2. Reread pp. 42–43. What materials did the Pueblo people use to build their homes?

_____

_____

3. What are *kachinas?*

_____

_____

4. Reread pp. 44–46. When did Spanish explorers first arrive in New Mexico?

_____

_____

5. How did life change when the Spanish arrived?

_____

_____

_____

Students analyze and respond to literary and informational text.

Name _____

DIRECTIONS Continue your opinion writing. Focus on organizing your ideas and details by grouping related information into well-organized paragraphs. Use linking words and phrases to connect details clearly.

_____

_____

_____

_____

_____

_____

_____

_____

Conventions

Coordinating Conjunctions Write your own sentences about *Three Native Nations: Of the Woodlands, Plains, and Desert.* Use commas with the coordinating conjunctions *and, but, yet, for,* and *so.*

1._____

_____

2._____

_____

3._____

_____

4._____

_____

 Students write routinely for a range of tasks, purposes, and audiences. Students practice various conventions of standard English.

Related Words

Words in Context Write words from the list to complete each sentence.

The **(1)** _____ of the course gave us specific

directions and was **(2)** _____ when certain
people began joking around.

I'm very **(3)** _____ to begin astronaut training.
I can't wait to get started.

The immense **(4)** _____ caused by the tornado
was difficult to witness.

It was quite the **(5)** _____, with many of the
town's finest on hand to witness the unveiling of the
20-foot statue.

His father's old watch has an **(6)** _____ on the
back from his great-grandfather.

The doctor will **(7)** _____ antibiotics for you if
necessary.

Are you interested in purchasing a 12-month **(8)**

_____ to the *New York Inquiry*?

The physicist discussed many interesting topics, including the color

(9) _____. But I was only a **(10)** _____, so I couldn't
ask any questions.

Word Bank
instructor
spectacle
destruction
subscription
unamused
excited
spectator
spectrum
inscription
prescribe

Students apply grade-level phonics and
word analysis skills.

Name _____

DIRECTIONS Use each word in a sentence.

vigil   obstacle   ceremonies   customs

_____

_____

_____

_____

_____

Write in Response to Reading

DIRECTIONS Revisit *The Longest Night* and *Three Native Nations: Of the Woodlands, Plains, and Desert*. In what ways are these two texts alike? In what ways are they different? Use examples from both texts to support your answer.

_____

_____

_____

_____

_____

_____

Students show contextual understanding of Benchmark Vocabulary. Students write routinely for a range of tasks, purposes, and audiences.

Name _____

DIRECTIONS Write a concluding paragraph for the opinion writing you started in Lesson 12. Make your topic clear by restating and summarizing your opinion in one or two sentences using new words. Include a clincher to add a fresh twist to your topic.

_____

_____

_____

_____

_____

Conventions

Spell Correctly Read each sentence. Cross out the misspelled word and write the corrected word on the line.

1. Mama was constantly preocupied with him.

_____

2. Others continued them in the guise of Christmas parties or charitabel giving.

_____

3. Write several sentences about your opinion piece. Remember to spell all words correctly.

_____

_____

_____

_____

Students write routinely for a range of tasks, purposes, and audiences. Students practice various conventions of standard English.

Benchmark Vocabulary

Name _____

DIRECTIONS Use each word in a sentence.

warrior   possessions   alliance

_____

_____

_____

_____

_____

Write in
Response to
Reading

DIRECTIONS Reread "Northwest Coast Peoples" and *Three Native Nations: Of the Woodlands, Plains, and Desert.* How are these texts similar to each other? Use examples from the texts to support your answer.

_____

_____

_____

_____

_____

_____

_____

_____

Students show contextual understanding
of Benchmark Vocabulary. Students write
routinely for a range of tasks, purposes, and
audiences.

Name _____

DIRECTIONS Using evidence from *The Longest Night*, "Northwest Coast Peoples," and *Three Native Nations: Of the Woodlands, Plains, and Desert*, follow the directions below.

1. Summarize each of the texts you have revisited on the lines below.

The Longest Night:

_____

_____

_____

"Northwest Coast Peoples":

_____

_____

_____

Three Native Nations: Of the Woodlands, Plains, and Desert:

_____

_____

_____

2. Compare and contrast each of the selections above. What do they have in common? How are they different? Use examples from the texts to support your answer.

_____

_____

_____

_____

_____

Students analyze and respond to literary and informational text.

Name _____

DIRECTIONS Edit and proofread the opinion writing piece you have been working on. Reread your writing several times, paying attention to different aspects of the editing process each time—ideas, transitional words and phrases, word choice, and so on. Remember to check your writing for grammar, capitalization, punctuation, and spelling.

_____

_____

_____

_____

_____

_____

_____

Conventions

Spell Correctly Use a dictionary to discover three unfamiliar words. Then write your own sentences using the words on the lines below.

1. _____

_____

2. _____

_____

3. _____

_____

Students write routinely for a range of tasks, purposes, and audiences. Students practice various conventions of standard English.

Name _____

DIRECTIONS Use each word in a sentence.

ritual   significant   social

_____

_____

_____

_____

_____

Write in
Response to
Reading

DIRECTIONS Reread pp. 8–12 of *The Longest Night*. Is there any information in "Northwest Coast Peoples" and *Three Native Nations: Of the Woodlands, Plains, and Desert* that directly supports pp. 8–12? Use examples from the text to support your answer.

_____

_____

_____

_____

_____

_____

Students show contextual understanding of Benchmark Vocabulary. Students write routinely for a range of tasks, purposes, and audiences.

Name _____

DIRECTIONS Publish and present the opinion writing you have been working on since Lesson 12. Use computer software to show your opinions and reasoning in a clear and interesting way. Include visuals to support your opinion.

Use a Dictionary Using a dictionary, look up five unfamiliar words from *The Longest Night*, "Northwest Coast Peoples," or *Three Native Nations: Of the Woodlands, Plains, and Desert* and define them on the lines below.

1. _____

_____

2. _____

_____

3. _____

_____

4. _____

_____

5. _____

_____

Students write routinely for a range of tasks, purposes, and audiences. Students practice various conventions of standard English.

Name _____

Multiple-Meaning Words

Word Bank

leaves	point	sharp	form	alarm
corner	story	forward	rose	start
force	storm	type	right	sport

DIRECTIONS Read the following sentences. Then circle the multiple-meaning word in each sentence.

1. Make a right turn at the next light, and look for the red door.

2. Amy can type over 100 words per minute.

3. My dogs worry when my mom leaves for work.

4. Don't you know that it's impolite to point at people?

5. She rose from her seat and sang a beautiful song for the crowd.

DIRECTIONS Read the definitions. Then write the list word that best fits both meanings.

6. _____ a shape **or** to make

7. _____ sudden fear **or** a warning device

8. _____ the place where two walls come together **or** to trap

9. _____ to begin **or** to jump in surprise or fright

10. _____ one floor of a building **or** a tale

11. _____ strong wind with heavy rain or snow **or** to show anger

12. _____ a game or contest **or** to wear

13. _____ ahead **or** bold

14. _____ having a thin, cutting edge **or** smart

15. _____ active power **or** to make someone act against his or her will

Students apply grade-level phonics and word analysis skills.

Name _____

DIRECTIONS Use each word in a sentence.

instruments   populated   energy

_____

_____

_____

_____

Write in Response to Reading

DIRECTIONS Reread pp. 8–9 of *Earthquakes*. Identify the type of earthquake that caused the change in the landscape. Then explain how the Earth's crust moves in this type of earthquake. Use evidence from the text to support your answer.

_____

_____

_____

_____

Students show contextual understanding of Benchmark Vocabulary. Students write routinely for a range of tasks, purposes, and audiences.

Name _____

DIRECTIONS Look at the photo on p. 4 in *Earthquakes* and reread the text on p. 5. Write a paragraph explaining whether the earthquake had some positive effects on the population or only negative effects. Support your opinion with reasons and evidence from the text and photo.

_____

_____

_____

_____

_____

Conventions

Progressive Verb Tenses Change the following sentence to past progressive: The ground is shaking and swaying. Then write three of your own sentences using progressive verb tenses.

1. _____

2. _____

_____

3. _____

_____

4. _____

_____

Students write routinely for a range of tasks, purposes, and audiences. Students practice various conventions of standard English.

Name _____

DIRECTIONS Use each word in a sentence.

dense   churns   strains   stresses

_____

_____

_____

_____

_____

_____

**Write in
Response to
Reading**

DIRECTIONS Reread pp. 10–13 of *Earthquakes*. Explain why most
of the earthquakes in the United States happen in California. What
information can you get from visuals to support your explanation? Use
evidence from the text to support your answer.

_____

_____

_____

_____

Students show contextual understanding
of Benchmark Vocabulary. Students write
routinely for a range of tasks, purposes, and
audiences.

Name _____

DIRECTIONS Using evidence from the text, answer the following questions about pp. 10–13 from *Earthquakes*.

1. Review the map on p. 11. On which coast do most major earthquakes occur?

   _____

   _____

   _____

2. What text evidence on p. 10 supports your answer?

   _____

   _____

   _____

3. What does the map on p. 12 show?

   _____

   _____

   _____

4. What do you learn about where most earthquakes occur? What text on p. 13 supports this fact?

   _____

   _____

   _____

Students analyze and respond to literary and informational text.

Name _____

DIRECTIONS Write an opinion paragraph telling which of the maps more effectively supports the topic of the text. Include at least two details from the text that support your opinion.

_____

_____

_____

_____

_____

Modal Auxiliaries Underline the modal auxiliary in the sentence below. Then write your own sentences using modal auxiliaries.

1. Earthquakes can occur anywhere there are stresses in underlying rocks.

2. _____

   _____

3. _____

   _____

4. _____

   _____

Students write routinely for a range of tasks, purposes, and audiences. Students practice various conventions of standard English.

Name _____

DIRECTIONS Use each word in a sentence.

violent   vertical

_____

_____

_____

Write in Response to Reading

DIRECTIONS Reread p. 17 of *Earthquakes*. Explain the movement of the San Andreas Fault during the 1906 earthquake. Use evidence from the text to support your answer.

_____

_____

_____

_____

_____

Students show contextual understanding of Benchmark Vocabulary. Students write routinely for a range of tasks, purposes, and audiences.

Name _____

Crater Lake

What images come to mind when you think of a volcano? Perhaps you think of molten lava spewing from one, or smoke pouring into the sky and covering the earth with ash. You probably wouldn't think of a fresh lake with the clearest and bluest water, would you?

Thousands of years ago the top of a volcano named Mount Mazama collapsed due to a powerful eruption. This resulted in a crater on top of the now inactive volcano. Lava sealed the bottom of the crater creating a basin. This basin gradually filled with water from rain and snowmelt. This crater is now called Crater Lake.

Nestled high in the Cascade Mountains of Oregon, Crater Lake is one of the deepest lakes in the world. The walls of old Mount Mazama tower above the lake, rising from 500 to 2,000 feet (152 to 610 meters). At its widest point, Crater Lake is about 6 miles (9 km) across.

Crater Lake is known for its blue color. The lake is so blue because it is very deep. In fact, this lake was once called Deep Blue Lake. The water is also nearly pure, which is a reason why the water is clear. Its purity and clarity are due to the fact that no rivers or streams flow into the lake.

If you visit Crater Lake, you will notice two islands: Wizard Island and Phantom Ship. You may also see a mountain hemlock log floating upright in the lake. What's so special about this log? It's known as the "Old Man" of Crater Lake, and it has been floating around the lake for over 100 years!

Today Crater Lake sits in Crater Lake National Park. Thanks to William Gladstone Steel, the lake and the surrounding area have been protected and preserved as a national park since 1902. Tourists can enjoy camping, fishing, and hiking during the warm months. However, from October to June, the park is buried under snow. No matter the season, Crater Lake is considered a place of great beauty.

Students read text closely to determine what the text says.

Gather Evidence. Underline text that describes how Crater Lake formed. Use evidence from the text to explain why *crater* is used in the name Crater Lake.

_____

Gather Evidence: Extend Your Ideas Focusing on the part of the text you identified, explain in your own words how water collects in Crater Lake.

_____

Ask Questions Write three questions you might ask a park ranger about Crater Lake.

_____

_____

_____

Ask Questions: Extend Your Ideas Write additional questions you have about Crater Lake.

_____

Make Your Case Circle passages that tell you that this text is informational rather than fictional.

Make Your Case: Extend Your Ideas Focusing on the part of the text you identified, explain in your own words why it's important to preserve Crater Lake.

_____

Students read text closely to determine what the text says.

Name _____

DIRECTIONS Write a brief explanation of what happened during the San Francisco earthquake of 1906, showing clear writing and organization of text. Then explain the most significant impact of the event, in your opinion. Use facts and details from the text to support your opinion.

_____

_____

_____

_____

_____

Conventions

Relative Adverbs Circle the relative adverb in the sentence below, and write whether the adverb indicates location, timing or situation, or reason. Then write your own sentences using relative adverbs.

1. Along the way, it slashes under houses and dams, across deserts and farms, and through towns and cities where more than 20 million people live.

_____

2. _____

_____

3. _____

_____

4. _____

_____

Students write routinely for a range of tasks, purposes, and audiences. Students practice various conventions of standard English.

Name _____

DIRECTIONS Use each word in a sentence.

detect   registers   immense   effects

_____

_____

_____

_____

_____

_____

Write in Response to Reading

DIRECTIONS Reread pp. 20–23 of *Earthquakes*. Which scale do you think is more effective—the Mercalli Intensity Scale or the Richter scale? Use evidence and details from the text to support your answer.

_____

_____

_____

_____

_____

Students show contextual understanding of Benchmark Vocabulary. Students write routinely for a range of tasks, purposes, and audiences.

Name _____

DIRECTIONS Using evidence from the text, answer the following questions about pp. 18–23 from *Earthquakes*.

1. Reread p. 18. What factors must scientists consider when comparing the size of two earthquakes?

   _____

   _____

2. What key words does the author use to explain how a *seismograph* works?

   _____

   _____

3. How many times more powerful is a magnitude-3 earthquake as opposed to a magnitude-2 earthquake?

   _____

   _____

4. Reread pp. 20–23. Look at the photographs. Would photographs be more helpful to a scientist using the Mercalli Intensity Scale or the Richter scale? Use evidence to support your answer.

   _____

   _____

5. Reread the final paragraph on p. 20 and on p. 23. What two events does the author compare? Use evidence from the text to support your answer.

   _____

   _____

Students analyze and respond to literary and informational text.

Name _____

DIRECTIONS Review the text and photographs on pp. 18–23 of *Earthquakes*. Write a paragraph in which you express an opinion about the comparisons the author makes between the Sumatra and San Francisco earthquakes. Do you think the text does a good job of comparing and contrasting these events? Would you organize the text differently and, if so, how? Use examples from the text to support your answer.

_____

_____

_____

_____

_____

Conventions

Capitalization Rewrite the sentence below using correct capitalization. Then write your own sentences about the buildings, people, or events in your neighborhood. Use correct capitalization.

1. The earthquake that shook the san francisco area in october 1989 measured 7.1 on the richter scale.

_____

_____

2. _____

_____

3. _____

_____

Students write routinely for a range of tasks, purposes, and audiences. Students practice various conventions of standard English.

Name _____

DIRECTIONS Use each word in a sentence.

miniature   erupted   foundations

_____

_____

_____

_____

_____

Write in
Response to
Reading

DIRECTIONS Reread the first paragraph on p. 29 of *Earthquakes*.
How does the simile on p. 29 help you understand what an underground
earthquake does to water? Use details from the text to support your
answer.

_____

_____

_____

_____

_____

Students show contextual understanding
of Benchmark Vocabulary. Students write
routinely for a range of tasks, purposes, and
audiences.

Name _____

DIRECTIONS Reread pp. 24–29 of *Earthquakes*. Write a paragraph describing the events caused by the 1964 earthquake in Anchorage, Alaska. Introduce the topic clearly, and explain why it was one of the most devastating earthquakes in U.S. history. Use facts and details from the text to develop and support your opinion.

_____

_____

_____

_____

_____

_____

Conventions

Adjectives Circle the adjective in the sentence below. Then write three of your own sentences using adjectives related to the five senses.

1. The ground rolled in huge waves.

2. _____

_____

3. _____

_____

4. _____

_____

Students write routinely for a range of tasks, purposes, and audiences. Students practice various conventions of standard English.

Name _____

Suffixes *-ian, -ist, -ism*

Word Bank

librarian	electrician	guitarist	tourism	pianist
optimism	athleticism	historian	comedian	activism
musician	moralism	politician	finalist	guardian

Missing Words

DIRECTIONS Complete the sentence by writing a list word.

1. She is a famous concert_____, and knows pianos inside and out.

   1. _____

2. I talked with the school_____ about a new book.

   2. _____

3. Many Caribbean islands have a thriving _____ industry.

   3. _____

4. It was comedy night and the young_____ was very funny.

   4. _____

5. She is a respected _____ who specializes in American history.

   5. _____

6. I respect your continued _____, as I'm often pessimistic.

   6. _____

7. Your permission slip must be signed by a legal _____.

   7. _____

8. The music teacher is a very talented_____.

   8. _____

9. Olympic athletes demonstrate tremendous _____.

   9. _____

10. I met the _____ of my favorite rock band!

    10. _____

Decode Words

DIRECTIONS Use *–ian, -ist,* or *-ism* with the root words below to create a list word.

11. final   11. _____
12. politic   12. _____
13. moral   13. _____
14. electric   14. _____
15. active   15. _____

Students apply grade-level phonics and word analysis skills.

Name _____

DIRECTIONS Use each word in a sentence.

slightest   predict

_____

_____

_____

DIRECTIONS Reread pp. 30–32 of *Earthquakes*. How might the study of earthquakes affect people's lives? Use details from the text to support your answer.

_____

_____

_____

_____

_____

Students show contextual understanding of Benchmark Vocabulary. Students write routinely for a range of tasks, purposes, and audiences.

Name _____

DIRECTIONS Many people choose to live in areas where earthquakes are common. Would you choose to live in an area that is earthquake-prone? Explain why or why not. Use evidence from the text to support your opinion, and use linking words to connect your reasons to the opinion. Include at least two prepositional phrases and underline the preposition.

_____

_____

_____

_____

_____

Conventions

Prepositional Phrases Underline the prepositional phrase in the sentence below. Then write three of your own sentences using prepositional phrases.

1. We need to know much more about earthquakes before we can predict an occurrence.

2. _____

_____

3. _____

_____

4. _____

_____

Students write routinely for a range of tasks, purposes, and audiences. Students practice various conventions of standard English.

Name _____

DIRECTIONS Use each word in a sentence.

tense   coaxed   agitated   frantic

_____

_____

_____

_____

_____

_____

**Write in
Response to
Reading**

DIRECTIONS Reread pp. 5–8 of *Quake!* How do dogs communicate
with people? Draw inferences from the text, and use examples to support
your answer.

_____

_____

_____

_____

_____

Students show contextual understanding
of Benchmark Vocabulary. Students write
routinely for a range of tasks, purposes,
and audiences.

DIRECTIONS Using evidence from the text, answer the following questions about pp. 5–8 from *Quake!*

1. Reread p. 7. How does the dog act?

_____

_____

2. Have you seen a dog act this way? Why might this happen?

_____

_____

3. What inference can you draw about the dog based on his behavior?

_____

_____

4. Do you think Jacob understands that something is wrong? Draw an inference using text evidence.

_____

_____

_____

5. What can you infer about Itzak's character? Use text evidence in your response.

_____

_____

_____

Students analyze and respond to literary and informational text.

Name _____

DIRECTIONS Write an opinion paragraph in which you answer the following question: How do you think Jacob feels about the dog? Use evidence from the text to support your answer.

_____

_____

_____

_____

_____

_____

_____

Commas and Quotation Marks Write dialogue based on the sources provided by your teacher. Remember to use commas and quotation marks correctly.

_____

_____

_____

_____

Students write routinely for a range of tasks, purposes, and audiences. Students practice various conventions of standard English.

Name _____

DIRECTIONS Use each word in a sentence.

realized   stampeded   careened

_____

_____

_____

_____

_____

Write in Response to Reading

DIRECTIONS Reread pp. 8–10 of *Quake!* List one example of figurative language. How does the author's use of figurative language make you want to read on? Use examples from the text to support your answer.

_____

_____

_____

_____

_____

_____

_____

Students show contextual understanding of Benchmark Vocabulary. Students write routinely for a range of tasks, purposes, and audiences.

Name _____

DIRECTIONS On p. 9, the author uses the simile, "Jacob's ears filled with a roar as loud as thunder." What does this simile mean? Write an opinion about whether or not this simile is effective. Explain why or why not. Use evidence from the text to support your answer.

_____

_____

_____

_____

_____

_____

_____

_____

Modal Auxiliaries Write three of your own sentences that use modal auxiliary verbs.

1. _____

_____

2. _____

_____

3. _____

_____

Students write routinely for a range of tasks, purposes, and audiences. Students practice various conventions of standard English.

DIRECTIONS Use each word in a sentence.

aimlessly   debris   emerged

_____

_____

_____

_____

Write in Response to Reading

DIRECTIONS Reread pp. 11–13 of *Quake!* Compare and contrast the setting in the Produce District before and after the aftershock. Use details from the text to support your answer.

_____

_____

_____

_____

Students show contextual understanding of Benchmark Vocabulary. Students write routinely for a range of tasks, purposes, and audiences.

Name _____

DIRECTIONS Using evidence from the text, answer the following questions about pp. 11–13 from *Quake!*

1. Describe the setting at the beginning of p. 11.

   _____

   _____

2. How did the people react to the earthquake?

   _____

   _____

3. How did the aftershock change the community? Did it change the setting? Use text evidence in your response.

   _____

   _____

   _____

   _____

4. What would have happened if the aftershock did not happen? Was the aftershock necessary to move the plot along?

   _____

   _____

   _____

   _____

Students analyze and respond to literary and informational text.

Name _____

DIRECTIONS What can you conclude about the setting following the earthquake in *Quake!*? Use evidence from the text to support an opinion about the scenes before and after the earthquake. Remember to explain how each piece of evidence relates to your opinion.

_____

_____

_____

_____

_____

Conventions

Frequently Confused Words Circle the words that are used incorrectly. Then write your own sentences using homophones.

1. Their pouring out of buildings, carrying they're belongings.

2. _____

_____

3. _____

_____

4. _____

_____

Students write routinely for a range of tasks, purposes, and audiences. Students practice various conventions of standard English.

Name _____

DIRECTIONS Use each word in a sentence.

casual   precaution

_____

_____

_____

_____

_____

Write in Response to Reading

DIRECTIONS Reread pp. 14–16 of *Quake!* Choose an example of sensory language, such as "collapsed into a pile of sticks" or "curtains of flames roaring across buildings." Identify the sense(s) and analyze the meaning or impact of the word choice. Use details from the text to support your answer.

_____

_____

_____

_____

_____

_____

_____

Students show contextual understanding of Benchmark Vocabulary. Students write routinely for a range of tasks, purposes, and audiences.

Name _____

DIRECTIONS Choose a descriptive phrase from *Quake!*. Write a paragraph that explains why it is effective and how other word choices would be less effective. Use examples from the text to support your answer.

_____

_____

_____

_____

_____

_____

Conventions

Order Adjectives Correctly Rewrite the sentence below, reordering the adjectives. Then write your own descriptive sentences about San Francisco after the 1906 earthquake. Remember to order your adjectives correctly.

1. Jacob handed back the yellow big jug.

2. _____

_____

3. _____

_____

4. _____

_____

Students write routinely for a range of tasks, purposes, and audiences.

Name _____

Latin Roots *aqua, dict*

Word Bank

dictionary	edict	predict	aquarium	indict
verdict	predicate	contradict	dictated	aquamarine
aquifer	aquatic	jurisdiction	dedicate	nonaquatic

Words in Context

DIRECTIONS Write a list word to complete each sentence.

1. Lions and giraffes are _____, meaning they live on land.

1. _____

2. An _____ is an area where fresh water can be found.

2. _____

3. Police officers dutifully patrol their _____.

3. _____

4. The jury will decide whether to _____ the suspect.

4. _____

5. Whales and squid are _____ animals.

5. _____

6. The author will _____ her new book to her children.

6. _____

7. Elaine loves studying fish, so her dad took her to the _____.

7. _____

8. I _____ my wishes, and she wrote them down for me.

8. _____

9. _____ refers to a light-bluish color or to a special stone.

9. _____

10. I used a _____ to look up unknown words.

10. _____

Definitions

DIRECTIONS Write the list word that matches each definition.

11. to make a statement of disagreement   11. _____
12. a jury's statement of guilt or innocence   12. _____
13. an official declaration   13. _____
14. to say what will happen in the future   14. _____
15. a part of a sentence   15. _____

Students apply grade-level phonics and word analysis skills.

Name _____

DIRECTIONS Use each word in a sentence.

unrecognizable   massive   intact   suggestion

_____

_____

_____

_____

_____

Write in Response to Reading

DIRECTIONS Reread pp. 16–20 of *Quake!* Should Jacob take the man's advice and start asking people in the street about his family? Why or why not? Use examples from the text to support your opinion.

_____

_____

_____

_____

_____

Students show contextual understanding of Benchmark Vocabulary. Students write routinely for a range of tasks, purposes, and audiences.

Name _____

DIRECTIONS Reread pp. 16–20 of *Quake!* Write an opinion paragraph about whether you think Jacob displays qualities of bravery. Explain why or why not. Use details and evidence from the text to support your opinion.

_____

_____

_____

_____

_____

_____

_____

_____

_____

Conventions

Coordinating Conjunctions Circle the coordinating conjunction that needs a comma before it.

1. Jacob searched the streets and buildings but he didn't see his father or his sister.

2. It sat on a large hill known as the Acropolis and it was the perfect place to hold a contest.

3. Jacob hurried to help it but four or five men had already reached its side.

4. Signs were hanging off storefronts and merchandise was scattered on the street.

Students write routinely for a range of tasks, purposes, and audiences. Students practice various conventions of standard English.

Name _____

DIRECTIONS Use each word in a sentence.

balancing   queasy   grimacing

_____

_____

_____

_____

**Write in
Response to
Reading**

DIRECTIONS Reread pp. 20–24 of *Quake!* Should Jacob have taken a
more active role in helping to rescue people from the collapsed buildings?
Why or why not? Use examples from the text to support your ideas.

_____

_____

_____

_____

_____

_____

Students show contextual understanding
of Benchmark Vocabulary. Students write
routinely for a range of tasks, purposes, and
audiences.

Name _____

DIRECTIONS Using evidence from the text, answer the following questions about pp. 17–24 of *Quake!*

1. Which word in the following sentence is a synonym for the word *spectators* on p. 18 and *sightseers* on p. 17?

   A knot of onlookers crowded around the men, pushing in to see the body as the men laid it down.

   _____

2. What does the word mean in context?

   _____

3. How is *onlookers* used differently from *spectators*?

   _____

   _____

   _____

4. In the text, how is *onlookers* used differently from *sightseers?*

   _____

   _____

   _____

   _____

5. Why did the author include the three synonyms?

   _____

   _____

Students analyze and respond to literary and informational text.

Name _____

DIRECTIONS Compare and contrast *Earthquakes* and *Quake!* Which text do you think offers a stronger account of an earthquake? Why? What elements in the text support the account best? Refer to your Venn Diagram, and choose the strongest text evidence to support your opinion. Create your graphic organizer in the space below.

_____

_____

_____

_____

_____

Conventions

Use and Order Adjectives Correctly Write a sentence about Jacob that uses the adjectives *little, daring*, and *curly-haired* in the correct order. Then write your own sentences about earthquakes using adjectives from the class brainstorm. Remember to order adjectives correctly.

1. _____

2. _____

 _____

3. _____

 _____

4. _____

 _____

Students write routinely for a range of tasks, purposes, and audiences. Students practice various conventions of standard English.

Name _____

DIRECTIONS Use each word in a sentence.

      erupted   foundations   agitated   frantic

_____

_____

_____

_____

_____

_____

Write in Response to Reading

DIRECTIONS Revisit pp. 4–32 of *Earthquakes* and pp. 5–24 of *Quake!*
Why is California at higher risk for earthquakes than other states in
America? Does the narrative help you understand this? Use examples from
both texts to support your answer.

_____

_____

_____

_____

_____

_____

_____

Students show contextual understanding
of Benchmark Vocabulary. Students write
routinely for a range of tasks, purposes,
and audiences.

Name _____

An Amazing Discovery

"Marcus, get your mother!" Aldo yelled. "I have something to show her!" It was a sizzling hot day. Aldo had risen early so he and his son could work in the coolness of the morning. They raised olives and grapes on a quaint farm in Italy in the early 1700s. These crops flourished in the fertile soil, made rich by volcanic ash.

That morning Aldo was digging a new well. As he was digging, his shovel hit something hard. He put the shovel down and started scraping at the dirt with his hands. When Marcus returned with his mother, Gina, they found Aldo looking into the eyes of a beautiful face. They helped him continue digging until they had uncovered an entire statue carved from marble.

"Aldo, my sister told me about a neighbor who found something like this when he dug his well," Gina said. "Do you think this is part of the same collection of ruins?"

The family met with their neighbors. Soon everyone was comparing items they had found in their own farm fields. People had unearthed coins, jewelry, bowls, and bricks. Some had even found bones.

Aldo and his neighbors worked their lands, and uncovered many other interesting artifacts buried in the soil. Soon, however, they were told to stop. They found out their farms were located near where the ancient city of Herculaneum had once been. To continue digging might damage the ruins and make it impossible to learn their secrets from the past.

Many centuries earlier, Herculaneum and Pompeii had been thriving cities. Yet one horrific day in A.D. 79, they were destroyed by a volcanic eruption. That day the nearby volcano known as Mount Vesuvius (ve SUE vee es) erupted. It buried the cities of Herculaneum and Pompeii under rock and ash. Thousands of people died, and everything in the cities was burned or buried.

Since the discovery of ruins that remain from the two cities, historians and archaeologists from all over the world have come to the area to excavate and see what else they can find. Today tourists flock to Pompeii and Herculaneum to see the ruins.

Students read text closely to determine what the text says.

Lesson 13

Name _____

Aldo and his neighbors often talked about what life must have been like in Herculaneum. They thought about how, if they had lived in the first century A.D., their farms would have been right in the middle of the city. Certainly they were glad to have lived instead at a different time, when their farms became a popular tourist attraction that drew visitors from around the world.

Gather Evidence Underline three details in the text that help you understand this is historical fiction.

Gather Evidence: Extend Your Ideas Based on what you underlined, when and where does this story take place?

_____

Ask Questions Circle three things in the text about Pompeii that interest you. What further questions do you have about Pompeii? On a separate sheet of paper, write three questions.

Ask Questions: Extend Your Ideas On a separate sheet of paper, write additional questions you have about Mount Vesuvius.

Make Your Case Draw a box around three details in the text about the eruption of Mount Vesuvius. On a separate sheet of paper, briefly explain why you would include these details in a summary. Use evidence from the text in your answer.

Make Your Case: Extend Your Ideas On a separate sheet of paper, write a summary of the eruption of Mount Vesuvius.

Students read text closely to determine what the text says.

Name _____

DIRECTIONS Write a draft of your opinion about which text provides a stronger account of an earthquake. Begin by describing each text's explanation of an earthquake, introducing each text one at a time and providing a summary of the text. Then compare and contrast each text's account. Choose the strongest text evidence from your Venn Diagram to support your opinion. Group related evidence together to organize your paragraphs

_____

_____

_____

_____

_____

Conventions

Progressive Verb Tenses Circle the progressive verb in each sentence. Then write two of your own sentences using progressive verb tenses.

1. "Don't worry, fella, we will be finding them soon."

2. Jacob was walking on the pile when he heard the dog yelp.

3. _____

_____

4. _____

_____

Students write routinely for a range of tasks, purposes, and audiences. Students practice various conventions of standard English.

Name _____

DIRECTIONS Use each word in a sentence.

transport   summons   represents   practical

_____

_____

_____

_____

_____

_____

Write in Response to Reading

DIRECTIONS Reread pp. 25–30 of "Earthshaker's Bad Day." What lesson has Poseidon learned by the end of the myth? Use details and context clues from the text to support your opinion.

_____

_____

_____

_____

Students show contextual understanding of Benchmark Vocabulary. Students write routinely for a range of tasks, purposes, and audiences.

Name _____

DIRECTIONS Using evidence from the text, answer the following questions about pp. 25–30 from "Earthshaker's Bad Day."

1. Reread the fourth paragraph on p. 26. What is the meaning of the word *bellowed*?

_____

_____

2. What textual clues help you figure out the meaning?

_____

_____

3. Reread the second paragraph on p. 30. What is the meaning of the word *fuming?*

_____

_____

4. What textual clues help you figure out the meaning?

_____

_____

5. Reread the fourth paragraph on p. 30. Why does everything return to normal when Poseidon calms down? What clues can you find in the text that might help to explain this?

_____

_____

_____

Students analyze and respond to literary and informational text.

Name _____

DIRECTIONS Revise the draft of the opinion piece you created in Lesson 13. Be sure your draft clearly states an opinion about which text offers a stronger account of an earthquake—*Earthquakes* or *Quake!* Change or add details as necessary in order to strengthen your writing.

_____

_____

_____

_____

_____

_____

Conventions

Use Prepositional Phrases Underline the prepositional phrases. Circle the prepositions. Then write your own sentences, underlining prepositional phrases and circling the prepositions.

1. He looked around the room at the lamps sitting on tables and the paintings hanging from the wall.

2. _____

_____

3. _____

_____

4. _____

_____

Students write routinely for a range of tasks, purposes, and audiences. Students practice various conventions of standard English.

Name _____

DIRECTIONS Use each word in a sentence.

commotion   decaying   torrent

_____

_____

_____

_____

_____

**Write in
Response to
Reading**

DIRECTIONS Reread pp. 31–36 of "The Monster Beneath the Sea."
How does Kashima do his best to make sure that the people of Japan will
be protected from earthquakes?

_____

_____

_____

_____

_____

Students show contextual understanding
of Benchmark Vocabulary. Students write
routinely for a range of tasks, purposes, and
audiences.

DIRECTIONS Review your opinion piece. Use different words when restating your opinion. Then review your conclusion and make sure that it is engaging and interesting. Remember that your concluding sentence should leave a strong impression on the reader.

_____

_____

_____

_____

_____

_____

_____

Conventions

Confusing Words Circle the correct word for each pair. Then write your own sentences using *there/they're/their* correctly.

1. The waves parted **to / two** allow his horses **threw / through**.

2. Look **hear / here**, I wouldn't worry **too / to** much about **their / they're** safety.

3. _____

_____

4. _____

_____

Students write routinely for a range of tasks, purposes, and audiences. Students practice various conventions of standard English.

Name _____

Prefixes *im-, in-*

immature	inefficient	insincere	impolite	imperfect
incapable	impartial	impossible	incorrect	indirect
improbable	impure	immortal	inadequate	impractical

DIRECTIONS For each definition, write a word from the list on the lines below.

1. not mature

2. not efficient

3. not sincere

4. not polite

5. not perfect

6. not mortal

7. not adequate

8. not capable

9. not partial

10. not possible

11. not correct

12. not direct

13. not practical

14. not probable

15. not pure

1. _____

2. _____

3. _____

4. _____

5. _____

6. _____

7. _____

8. _____

9. _____

10. _____

11. _____

12. _____

13. _____

14. _____

15. _____

Students apply grade-level phonics and word analysis skills.

Name _____

DIRECTIONS Use each word in a sentence.

populated   transport   propelled

_____

_____

_____

_____

DIRECTIONS Think about the following texts— "Earthshaker's Bad Day" and "The Monster Beneath the Sea." Would reading either of these myths teach a reader real facts about the experience of being in an earthquake? Use examples from the texts to support your answer.

_____

_____

_____

_____

Students show contextual understanding of Benchmark Vocabulary. Students write routinely for a range of tasks, purposes, and audiences.

Name _____

DIRECTIONS Return to the opinion you have been writing. Make sure that your writing includes a clear and focused opinion about which text you believe provides the strongest account of an earthquake. Remember that your opinion should be supported with facts and details from the text. Use linking words to connect your opinions and reasons. Remember to include your revised conclusion from the previous lesson.

_____

_____

_____

_____

_____

Conventions

Relative Adverbs Circle the relative adverb, and underline the noun it modifies. Then write your own sentences using relative adverbs. Be sure to circle the relative adverb and underline the noun it modifies.

1. Kashima is the only god who can protect us from Namazu.

2. _____

_____

3. _____

_____

4. _____

_____

Students write routinely for a range of tasks, purposes, and audiences. Students practice various conventions of standard English.

Name _____

DIRECTIONS Use each word in a sentence.

immense   effects   massive   intact   summons   represents   torrent

_____

_____

_____

_____

_____

Write in Response to Reading

DIRECTIONS Why do you think people use myths instead of facts to explain natural events? Include ideas about the text structure of myths and authors' purposes in your answer. Use details from the texts to support your answer.

_____

_____

_____

_____

Students show contextual understanding of Benchmark Vocabulary. Students write routinely for a range of tasks, purposes, and audiences.

Name _____

DIRECTIONS Using evidence from the text, answer the following questions about *Earthquakes,* "Earthshaker's Bad Day," and "The Monster Beneath the Sea."

1. Which two texts are similar in structure?

_____

_____

2. How are they similar?

_____

_____

3. Which texts are factual? Which are imaginary?

_____

_____

4. How does the purpose of "Earthshaker's Bad Day" and "The Monster Beneath the Sea" differ from *Earthquakes?*

_____

_____

5. How are the visuals in *Earthquakes* different from "Earthshaker's Bad Day"?

_____

_____

Students analyze and respond to literary and informational text.

Name _____

DIRECTIONS Edit and proofread the comparisons you began in Lesson 12. Make sure you have used proper punctuation when citing the titles of sources and quoting from the sources. Then verify that you have properly capitalized the text titles and names of places and people from the texts.

_____

_____

_____

_____

_____

_____

_____

Conventions

Use Commas Before Coordinating Conjunctions Place a comma in the correct spot in each sentence below. Then write your own sentences using the coordinating conjunctions *and, but*, or *so*.

1. The chances of an earthquake hurting you are low so don't worry.

2. Poseidon shook with rage and his voice boomed across the sky.

3. _____

_____

4. _____

_____

Students write routinely for a range of tasks, purposes, and audiences. Students practice various conventions of standard English.

Name _____

DIRECTIONS Use each word in a sentence.

detect   registers   aimlessly   emerged

practical   commotion   decaying

_____

_____

_____

_____

_____

_____

_____

_____

Write in Response to Reading

DIRECTIONS Do you think reading fiction about real-world events helps you understand the events better? Use examples from at least two of the texts to support your ideas.

_____

_____

_____

_____

Students show contextual understanding of Benchmark Vocabulary. Students write routinely for a range of tasks, purposes, and audiences.

Name _____

DIRECTIONS Publish and present the comparison you wrote in Lesson 12. Begin by drafting a plan for your presentation. Then, alter your writing as necessary. Check for short, choppy sentences and rewrite them by forming compound sentences. Finally, present your writing to the class.

_____

_____

_____

_____

_____

_____

Conventions

Compound Sentences Rewrite the following as a compound sentence joined by a coordinating conjunction.

1. Most earthquakes are too small to be noticed by people. Scientific instruments are sensitive enough to record them.

_____

_____

_____

2. He was trapped. He was unable to create even the smallest earthquake.

_____

_____

Students write routinely for a range of tasks, purposes, and audiences. Students practice various conventions of standard English.

Name _____

Greek and Latin Prefixes *trans-, tele-*

Word Bank

television	telegraph	translucent	transcend
transaction	transform	teleprompter	transcript
transport	telescope	translate	transcribe

DIRECTIONS Write the list word that best fits into each group.

1. change, morph, _____

2. cartoon, remote control, _____

3. payment, deal, _____

4. universe, lens, _____

5. write down, type out, _____

1. _____

2. _____

3. _____

4. _____

5. _____

DIRECTIONS Write the list word that best completes each sentence.

6. Your grades and classes are listed on your _____.

7. Modern airplanes _____ millions of passengers around the world.

8. I spoke very little Spanish, so I hired someone to _____.

9. Morse code, a series of dots and dashes, was sent by _____.

10. The mayor's speech was visible on the _____.

11. _____ means to go beyond something.

12. If light can easily pass through something, then it is _____.

6. _____

7. _____

8. _____

9. _____

10. _____

11. _____

12. _____

Students apply grade-level phonics and word analysis skills.

Name _____

DIRECTIONS Use each word in a sentence.

volcano   spewed   atmosphere

_____

_____

_____

_____

_____

Write in Response to Reading

DIRECTIONS Reread pp. 4–5 of *Anatomy of a Volcanic Eruption.*
Describe what happened in Iceland on April 14, 2010. Use evidence
from the text to support your answer.

_____

_____

_____

_____

Students show contextual understanding
of Benchmark Vocabulary. Students write
routinely for a range of tasks, purposes,
and audiences.

Name _____

DIRECTIONS Reread pp. 4–5 of *Anatomy of a Volcanic Eruption*. Then write an informative/explanatory paragraph that explains how a famous volcano was formed. Use details from the text to support your answer.

_____

_____

_____

_____

_____

Conventions

Complete Sentences Identify whether the subject or predicate is missing. Change the fragment to a complete sentence. Then write your own complete sentences about the eruption in Iceland.

1. began to flow

_____

2. _____

_____

3. _____

_____

4. _____

_____

Students write routinely for a range of tasks, purposes, and audiences. Students practice various conventions of standard English.

Greek Prefixes *amphi-, anti-*

Word Bank

amphibious	anticipating	antibiotic
amphibian	antifreeze	antitheft
antidote	antibody	antivirus
antipathy	antithesis	amphitheater

DIRECTIONS Write the list word that best completes each sentence.

1. The doctor gave me an _____ for my illness.

1. _____

2. _____ means a strong feeling of dislike.

2. _____

3. The direct opposite of someone or something is the _____ of that person or thing.

3. _____

4. I saw a famous play at the _____ in the park.

4. _____

5. An _____ vehicle can operate on both land and water.

5. _____

6. He was bitten by a snake, but fortunately they had an _____.

6. _____

7. An _____ is what helps your body fight infection.

7. _____

8. The salamander is an _____.

8. _____

9. Many vehicles come with _____ devices.

9. _____

10. I downloaded new _____ software for my computer.

10. _____

11. She was _____ having a bad time at the dentist office.

11. _____

12. _____ prevents important engine parts from freezing.

12. _____

Students apply grade-level phonics and word analysis skills.

Name _____

DIRECTIONS Use each word in a sentence.

interior   pressure   collide   disruption

_____

_____

_____

_____

_____

_____

Write in Response to Reading

DIRECTIONS Reread pp. 6–13 of *Anatomy of a Volcanic Eruption*. Explain how the island chain of Hawaii was formed. Then suggest a visual that would best illustrate how the islands were formed.

_____

_____

_____

_____

_____

_____

_____

Students show contextual understanding of Benchmark Vocabulary. Students write routinely for a range of tasks, purposes, and audiences.

DIRECTIONS Using evidence from the text, answer the following questions about the cover, Table of Contents, introduction on pp. 4–5, and the glossary from *Anatomy of a Volcanic Eruption*.

1. What appears in the Table of Contents? What clues from the cover and the Table of Contents tell you that this book is about volcanoes?

_____

_____

_____

2. What is covered on pp. 4–5?

_____

_____

3. Why do you think the author included this information as an introduction?

_____

_____

4. What kinds of text features appear in the glossary on p. 46?

_____

_____

5. Can you tell what the genre of the book is by the Table of Contents and pp. 4–5? Explain your answer.

_____

_____

_____

Students analyze and respond to literary and informational text.

Name _____

DIRECTIONS Create a diagram of an active volcano. Include labels and boxed text to provide additional information about the diagram. Use information from the text to support your answer.

Relative Adverbs Circle the relative adverbs in the sentences below. Then write your own sentences using relative adverbs.

1. The Ring of Fire is where the Pacific Ocean meets with all of the continental plates surrounding it.

2. The area where the sea floor is spreading is called the Mid-Atlantic Ridge.

3. _____

_____

4. _____

_____

Students write routinely for a range of tasks, purposes, and audiences. Students practice various conventions of standard English.

Name _____

DIRECTIONS Use each word in a sentence.

originated   expected   structures

_____

_____

_____

_____

_____

**Write in
Response to
Reading**

DIRECTIONS Reread pp. 16–19 of *Anatomy of a Volcanic Eruption.*
Which type of volcano do you think is most interesting? What key details
about this type of volcano interest you the most? Use evidence from the
text to support your answer.

_____

_____

_____

_____

_____

_____

_____

_____

Students show contextual understanding
of Benchmark Vocabulary. Students write
routinely for a range of tasks, purposes,
and audiences.

The Layering Effect

The surface of Earth is constantly being changed. Rocks are constantly being formed, destroyed, or changed. The changes to Earth's surface might be caused by erosion, weathering, volcanic eruptions, or the actions of humans. Do you think there is a lot of activity on Earth's surface? What happens deep inside the Earth can affect what happens where we live.

The layer we walk and live on is called the crust. It is Earth's thinnest layer. There are two kinds of crust, continental crust and oceanic crust. Continental crust makes up all of Earth's land. Oceanic crust lies beneath most of the ocean floor. The thickest part of the crust is about 25 miles (40 km) deep. The thinnest part is about 3 miles (5 km) deep. This leaner layer is at the bottom of the ocean.

Below the crust is a layer called the mantle. It is the thickest layer— almost 1,864 miles (3,000 km) thick and made up of nearly solid rock. It is much hotter than the crust. In fact, it is so hot that rocks can move, bend, and even melt! Sometimes, the melted rock can flow onto the crust as lava and volcanoes form.

The top of the mantle and the crust above it form the lithosphere. Under the mantle, in Earth's center is a super-hot core. The core is made of iron and nickel: the outer part of the core is liquid and the inner part is solid. Scientists think that heat rising up from the core may be one cause of earthquakes. They also think the inner core spins in place. It creates an invisible magnetic shield that protects us from the sun.

The lithosphere covers Earth in a thin layer, which is split into sections called plates. The plates float on the molten rock of the mantle. Earth's plates are slowly moving. Sometimes the plates grind together, and sometimes they move apart. Some of the changes occur slowly, such as the formation of mountains. A change that happens quickly can cause an earthquake. The places where plates meet are often where earthquakes strike, mountains form, and volcanoes erupt.

Scientists keep digging to learn how Earth's lower layers affect our world and what they teach us about the past. They can use Earth's layers to learn about the ages of fossils by studying the layers in which they were found.

Students read text closely to determine what the text says.

Name _____

Gather Evidence Draw a box around the layers of the Earth. Briefly explain what the text says about each.

_____

_____

Gather Evidence: Extend Your Ideas Focusing on the layers you identified, explain how one of these layers can change Earth's surface.

_____

_____

Ask Questions Underline text that a scientist might find interesting. What is one question a scientist might have about Earth's layers?

_____

_____

Ask Questions: Extend Your Ideas Write two additional questions you have about earthquakes.

_____

_____

Make Your Case Which layer do you find the most interesting? Explain why, using information from the text.

_____

_____

Make Your Case: Extend Your Ideas Circle a challenging word from the text, and give the definition that best fits the context of the text.

_____

_____

Students read text closely to determine what the text says.

Name _____

DIRECTIONS Write an informative/explanatory paragraph that explains what a volcanologist does. Remember to group related information and use proper headings.

_____

_____

_____

_____

_____

Conventions

Use Relative Adverbs Circle the relative adverb in the sentence below, and write whether the relative adverb tells the location, timing or situation, or reason. Then write your own sentences using relative adverbs.

1. Lava Domes form when the lava that pushes out of the conduit is too thick and dusty to move a great distance.

_____

2. _____

_____

3. _____

_____

4. _____

_____

Students write routinely for a range of tasks, purposes, and audiences. Students practice various conventions of standard English.

Name _____

DIRECTIONS Use each word in a sentence.

       categorize   explodes   intervals   occurred

_____

_____

_____

_____

_____

_____

Write in Response to Reading

DIRECTIONS Reread pp. 22–23 of *Anatomy of a Volcanic Eruption*.
Write a paragraph summarizing the information on these pages. Use
information from the web you created that shows the most important ideas
on these pages support your answer.

_____

_____

_____

_____

_____

_____

_____

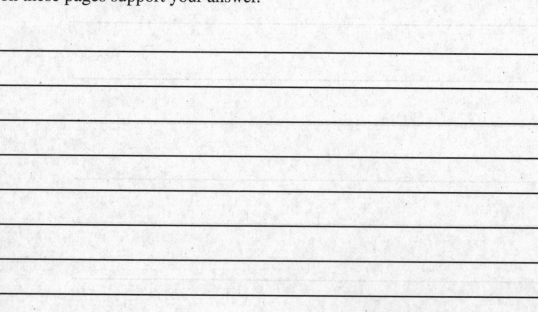

Students show contextual understanding
of Benchmark Vocabulary. Students write
routinely for a range of tasks, purposes,
and audiences.

Name _____

DIRECTIONS Write several paragraphs about the volcanic eruption you chose. Organize your information in a logical way to clearly show your readers what happened.

_____

_____

_____

_____

_____

_____

_____

Conventions

Relative Pronouns Circle the relative pronouns in the sentences below. Underline the noun each describes. Then write your own sentences using relative pronouns. Use information from pp. 20–27 of *Anatomy of a Volcanic Eruption*.

1. They have quick-moving lava flows that don't usually send out much ash.

2. A surtseyan eruption is a volcanic eruption that occurs underwater or very close to the surface of the water.

3. _____

_____

4. _____

_____

 Students write routinely for a range of tasks, purposes, and audiences. Students practice various conventions of standard English.

Benchmark Vocabulary

Name _____

DIRECTIONS Use each word in a sentence.

investigations   diverted

_____

_____

_____

Write in Response to Reading

DIRECTIONS Reread p. 31 of *Anatomy of a Volcanic Eruption*. What is the meaning of the word *tiltmeters?* Write an opinion about whether the use of this term is helpful and effective in helping you understand volcanology. Use details from the text to support your opinion.

_____

_____

_____

_____

_____

_____

Students show contextual understanding of Benchmark Vocabulary. Students write routinely for a range of tasks, purposes, and audiences.

Name _____

DIRECTIONS Using evidence from the text, answer the following questions about pp. 28–31 of *Anatomy of a Volcanic Eruption*.

1. What kind of sentence is, "The study of volcanoes is called volcanology"?

   _____

2. Reread p. 29. What is the meaning of the word *seismograph*?

   _____

3. What clues on p. 29 could help you find out what a *seismograph* is?

   _____

   _____

4. Reread the fourth paragraph on p. 30. What does the word *convergent* mean?

   _____

   _____

5. Write something you learned about types of volcanoes or volcanic structures. Include domain-specific vocabulary.

   _____

   _____

   _____

   _____

   _____

   _____

Students analyze and respond to literary and informational text.

Name _____

DIRECTIONS Write several paragraphs about a volcanology tool. Tell why it's important and explain how it works. Use facts, details, and domain-specific vocabulary to support your answer.

_____

_____

_____

_____

_____

_____

_____

_____

_____

_____

Conventions

Modal Auxiliaries Underline the modal auxiliary in the sentence below. Then write your own sentences with verb phrases, using the modal auxiliaries *can, may, might,* or *must*.

1. Earthquakes can occur before, during, and after volcanic eruptions.

2. _____

_____

3. _____

_____

4. _____

_____

 Students write routinely for a range of tasks, purposes, and audiences. Students practice various conventions of standard English.

Name _____

Antonyms, Synonyms

Word Bank

distrust	disagreeable	retirement	white
whiskers	disorder	wharf	think
whisper	trunk	questionable	displacement
misdialed	among	declaration	shrink

DIRECTIONS Write the list word that has the opposite, or nearly the opposite, meaning as the word or phrase.

1. shout

1. _____

2. pleasant

2. _____

3. shipshape

3. _____

4. have faith in

4. _____

5. black

5. _____

6. grow

6. _____

7. certain

7. _____

DIRECTIONS Write the list word that has the same, or nearly the same, meaning as the word or phrase.

8. beard

8. _____

9. ponder

9. _____

10. called the wrong number

10. _____

11. career's end

11. _____

12. relocation

12. _____

13. dock

13. _____

14. statement

14. _____

15. with

15. _____

16. box

16. _____

Students apply grade-level phonics and word analysis skills.

Name _____

DIRECTIONS Use each word in a sentence.

benefits   resources   nutrients

_____

_____

_____

_____

_____

DIRECTIONS Reread p. 33 of *Anatomy of a Volcanic Eruption*. Create a graphic organizer to help explain a cause and effect from this section. Then use information from your graphic organizer to explain the cause and effect.

_____

_____

_____

_____

_____

Students show contextual understanding of Benchmark Vocabulary. Students write routinely for a range of tasks, purposes, and audiences.

DIRECTIONS Reread pp. 32–35 of *Anatomy of a Volcanic Eruption*. Write several paragraphs explaining the benefits and dangers of volcanic eruptions. Include a diagram with a caption and labels to illustrate the information in your paragraph. Use details from the text to support your answer.

_____

_____

_____

_____

_____

Conventions

Punctuating Quotations Use a comma and quotation marks to punctuate the sentence correctly. Then quote two sentences from *Anatomy of a Volcanic Eruption* using correct punctuation.

1. In *Anatomy of a Volcanic Eruption*   the author writes   Though they are sometimes violent and destructive, volcanoes provide many benefits for our planet.

2. _____

_____

3. _____

_____

Students write routinely for a range of tasks, purposes, and audiences. Students practice various conventions of standard English.

Name _____

DIRECTIONS Use each word in a sentence.

residents   survivors   refuge

_____

_____

_____

_____

Write in Response to Reading

DIRECTIONS The author includes maps, photographs, captions, headings, and a quotation as text features in this section. How do these text features help add additional descriptive details to the text? Use details from the text to support your answer.

_____

_____

_____

_____

Students show contextual understanding of Benchmark Vocabulary. Students write routinely for a range of tasks, purposes, and audiences.

Name _____

DIRECTIONS   Using evidence from the text, answer the following questions about pp. 36–41 of *Anatomy of a Volcanic Eruption*.

1. What details on pp. 38–39 relate to the sense of sight?

_____

_____

2. What details on pp. 38–39 relate to the sense of hearing?

_____

3. How do the details on pp. 40–41 help you visualize the events?

_____

_____

_____

4. What details on p. 41 help you visualize the tsunami?

_____

_____

_____

5. Which sense do the details about the tsunami relate to?

_____

_____

_____

Students analyze and respond to literary and informational text.

Name _____

DIRECTIONS Reread pp. 36–41 of *Anatomy of a Volcanic Eruption*.
Work with your partner to write research questions for an interview with
a volcanologist that begin with *who, what, where, when, why*, or *how*.
Avoid writing questions that can be answered with a *yes* or *no*. Then do
additional research about the topic on the Internet or at the school library.

_____

_____

_____

_____

_____

Conventions

Correct Fragments Rewrite the fragments below to make complete
sentences.

1. towered in the distance

_____

2. loomed over us

_____

3. into the crater

_____

4. as there is a fault nearby

_____

Students write routinely for a range of
tasks, purposes, and audiences. Students
practice various conventions of standard
English.

Benchmark Vocabulary

Name _____

DIRECTIONS Use each word in a sentence.

contained   experiencing   tremors

_____

_____

_____

_____

_____

Write in Response to Reading

DIRECTIONS Today, many people hike on Mount St. Helens. Do you think this is a good idea? What facts from the author's purpose to inform make you think this way? Use evidence from the text to support your answer.

_____

_____

_____

_____

_____

Students show contextual understanding of Benchmark Vocabulary. Students write routinely for a range of tasks, purposes, and audiences.

Name _____

DIRECTIONS Write an informative/explanatory draft about what life is like for people living in the shadow of a volcano. Use pp. 44–45 of *Anatomy of a Volcanic Eruption* and additional sources to find facts and quotations. Choose facts and quotations that your reader will find interesting.

_____

_____

_____

_____

Conventions

Correct Run-Ons Correct the following sentence in three ways: by making two separate sentences, by adding a comma and coordinating conjunction, and by adding a semicolon.

The eruption reaches its peak cities that are hundreds of miles away from Mount St. Helens report experiencing total darkness just hours after the blast.

1. _____

   _____

2. _____

   _____

3. _____

   _____

Students write routinely for a range of tasks, purposes, and audiences. Students practice various conventions of standard English.

Name _____

DIRECTIONS Use the word in a sentence.

seriously

_____

_____

DIRECTIONS Reread pp. 37–45 of *Escape from Pompeii*. How does the author's word choice set and change the mood of the story? Use details from the text to support your answer.

_____

_____

_____

_____

_____

_____

_____

_____

Students show contextual understanding
of Benchmark Vocabulary. Students write
routinely for a range of tasks, purposes, and
audiences.

DIRECTIONS Using evidence from the text, answer the following questions about pp. 37–45 of *Escape from Pompeii*.

1. Which words help you understand what the town is like in the last paragraph on p. 39?

_____

_____

2. Which words affect the mood in the first paragraph on p. 43?

_____

_____

3. How does the word *laughing* in the last paragraph on p. 43 affect the mood?

_____

_____

4. How does the mood change on p. 44? Which words show this change in mood?

_____

_____

_____

_____

5. Why do you think the author includes words that describe the mood?

_____

_____

_____

Students analyze and respond to literary and informational text.

DIRECTIONS Plan and draft travel brochures to inform travelers about ancient Pompeii. Use facts, definitions, descriptive details, precise vocabulary, proper formatting, and illustrations to support your answer.

_____

_____

_____

_____

_____

_____

_____

_____

Conventions

Progressive Verb Tenses Underline the progressive verb in the sentence below. Then write your own sentences using progressive verb tenses.

1. One hot August day, Dion took Tranio through a shady passage into one of Pompeii's two theaters on the edge of the city, where a pantomime was being rehearsed.

2. _____

_____

3. _____

_____

Students write routinely for a range of tasks, purposes, and audiences. Students practice various conventions of standard English.

Name _____

DIRECTIONS Use each word in a sentence.

anxious   desperately   quivered

_____

_____

_____

_____

**Write in
Response to
Reading**

DIRECTIONS Reread pp. 46–54 of *Escape from Pompeii*. Describe
Tranio's character traits using his own thoughts, words, and actions to
support your description. How do these traits support his point of view?
Use details from the text to support your answer.

_____

_____

_____

_____

_____

_____

_____

Students show contextual understanding
of Benchmark Vocabulary. Students write
routinely for a range of tasks, purposes,
and audiences.

Name _____

DIRECTIONS Conduct research, and then write to inform readers about the events at Pompeii. Use linking words and phrases to connect ideas. Use sequence charts with sections for *Beginning, Middle*, and *End* to organize information from your K-W-L Charts in time order. Revisit the text to look for ideas.

_____

_____

_____

_____

_____

_____

Consult References to Spell Words Cross out the misspelled word, and write the correct word on the line. Then write a list of strategies you can use for finding unknown words in the dictionary.

1. Everyone was showting.

_____

2. _____

_____

_____

_____

_____

Students write routinely for a range of tasks, purposes, and audiences. Students practice various conventions of standard English.

Words from French

DIRECTIONS Circle the eight spelling errors in the school poster. Write the words correctly.

Our New After-School Programs

Learn to Ski!
- 2 Saturday Ski Trips
- Meet at 8:00 AM in the parking gerage
- delaxe package includes lift ticket!
- no parashute necessary!

Learn to Cook!
- create your own manu • hamburgers, pasta, quishe, and more! • meet in the caffé at 3:30! • free supermarket koupons!

Learn to Play Baseball!
- Meet the Cubs maskot
- Batting Cage!
- Infield and Outfield Drills!

Sign up at the kiosk outside the office.
Bring a permission form from your parents.

Word Bank

| coupon |
| menu |
| café |
| deluxe |
| parachute |
| mascot |
| garage |
| quiche |

1. _____ 2. _____

3. _____ 4. _____

5. _____ 6. _____

7. _____

8. _____

Frequently Misspelled Words

address

experience

DIRECTIONS Circle the correct spelling of the list word. Write the word.

9. I lost the _____ of my friend's summer camp.

    address   adress   addres

9. _____

10. It's important to have _____.

    experryence   experience   exxperience

10. _____

Students apply grade-level phonics and word analysis skills.

Lesson 11

Benchmark Vocabulary

Name _____

DIRECTIONS Use each word in a sentence.

originate   expected   structures   seriously   quivered

_____

_____

_____

_____

_____

_____

_____

_____

Write in Response to Reading

DIRECTIONS Revisit *Anatomy of a Volcanic Eruption* and *Escape from Pompeii*. Which secondhand account gives you better, more reliable information? Use evidence from both texts to support your answer.

_____

_____

_____

_____

_____

_____

_____

Students show contextual understanding of Benchmark Vocabulary. Students write routinely for a range of tasks, purposes, and audiences.

Name _____

DIRECTIONS Write an informative/explanatory paragraph to address this question: How can we reduce the impact of a natural Earth process on humans? Begin with an introduction that identifies your topic. Then introduce each fact you researched in a logical order.

_____

_____

_____

_____

_____

_____

_____

Conventions

Modal Auxiliaries Circle the modal auxiliary in the sentence below. Then write your own sentences using modal auxiliaries.

1. Scientists can try to predict tsunamis using sensors.

2. _____

_____

3. _____

_____

4. _____

_____

Students write routinely for a range of tasks, purposes, and audiences. Students practice various conventions of standard English.

Name _____

DIRECTIONS Use each word in a sentence.

collapsed   networks   evacuation

_____

_____

_____

_____

_____

**Write in
Response to
Reading**

DIRECTIONS Reread pp. 8–9 of *A Tsunami Unfolds*. How does the
earthquake that struck Japan in 2011 compare with other powerful
earthquakes? Use details from the text to support your answer.

_____

_____

_____

_____

_____

Students show contextual understanding
of Benchmark Vocabulary. Students write
routinely for a range of tasks, purposes, and
audiences.

Name _____

DIRECTIONS Using evidence from the text, answer the following questions about pp. 4–11 of *A Tsunami Unfolds*.

1. Reread pp. 6–7. What was Yumi doing when the earthquake struck?

   _____

   _____

2. Who developed the Richter scale? When was it first developed?

   _____

3. Reread pp. 10–11. What is a *tsunami*?

   _____

   _____

4. How fast can a *tsunami* travel?

   _____

   _____

5. Why did experts consider Japan to be the best-prepared country to deal with tsunamis?

   _____

   _____

   _____

   _____

Students analyze and respond to literary and informational text.

Lesson 12

Name _____

DIRECTIONS Revisit *Anatomy of a Volcanic Eruption* and pp. 4–11 of *A Tsunami Unfolds*. Write two paragraphs explaining how forces of nature, such as volcanoes, earthquakes, and tsunamis affect land. Use examples from both texts to support your answer.

_____

_____

_____

_____

_____

_____

_____

Conventions

Use Commas Before Coordinating Conjunctions Combine the sentences below to form a compound sentence. Be sure to add a coordinating conjunction and comma where needed. Then write your own compound sentence that uses a comma and coordinating conjunction.

1. Pieces of rock could be carried downhill by rainwater. They could slide down in an avalanche.

   _____

   _____

2. _____

   _____

Students write routinely for a range of tasks, purposes, and audiences. Students practice various conventions of standard English.

Name _____

DIRECTIONS Use each word in a sentence.

evacuate   scrambling   monitoring   broadcast

_____

_____

_____

_____

_____

_____

**Write in
Response to
Reading**

DIRECTIONS Reread pp. 16–17 of *A Tsunami Unfolds*. What is a nuclear meltdown? Use details from the text to support your answer.

_____

_____

_____

_____

Students show contextual understanding of Benchmark Vocabulary. Students write routinely for a range of tasks, purposes, and audiences.

Name _____

Rocking It

"Patrick, your room looks like a rock quarry," Mom said as she stepped over a pile of rocks.

"I know," Patrick said. "It's awesome!"

"It's a neat collection, Patrick, but it's taking over your room. Maybe it's time to start weeding some out."

"I wouldn't know which ones to discard," Patrick complained.

That afternoon Patrick and his mom were gardening when their neighbor Mrs. Simpson stopped by. Mrs. Simpson worked at the nature center and always had interesting facts to share about plants.

"What are you planting today?" she asked.

Patrick spoke up. "Mom's planting peppers, and I'm digging for rocks."

"Patrick's rock collection keeps expanding, and he's running out of space to store them," Mom added. "Why don't you show Mrs. Simpson your collection, Patrick?"

Patrick led Mrs. Simpson his room. Mrs. Simpson's eyes grew big when she saw all the rocks.

"Wow, Patrick, this is quite a collection!" she said. "Do you know what kind of rocks you have?"

"No, they're just rocks," Patrick said. "My mom just wants me to get rid of some of them."

"Well, it may be interesting to know which minerals are in those rocks. Minerals are the building blocks of rocks. Minerals can be identified by their physical properties, such as color, hardness, luster, and streak."

"That sounds really cool, Mrs. Simpson. I'd love to learn how to identify minerals."

"Rocks also go through many changes. Over time, rocks can *erode* from storms and water currents. Look at this one that you have here. Did you get it by the shoreline? You can tell that it broke off from a larger rock during the process of wave erosion."

"How did you know that, Mrs. Simpson?" Patrick asked.

Students read text closely to determine what the text says.

"Patrick, come to the nature center. You can look through field guides to see what you have. You can learn about processes like erosion and weathering, as well as the three different types of rock: **igneous, sedimentary, metamorphic.** You can also learn about the rock cycle. Once you have learned more about the rocks, you may find some to get rid of. A good rock collector learns to be particular about his rocks."

"AWESOME!" said Patrick. "I didn't realize there was so much to collecting rocks. I'll see you at the nature center!"

Properties of Minerals

Color	Minerals come in colors that range from clear to pink, red, blue, green, and black.
Hardness	Hardness is measured on Mohs scale. The scale grades minerals from one to ten.
Luster	Minerals can be dull or shiny. There are some you can see through and others you cannot see through.
Streak	Streak refers to the color of a mineral or what its powder color is.

Gather Evidence Circle some words in the text that the author draws attention to.

Gather Evidence: Extend Your Ideas Explain how the author draws attention to the words you circled.

_____

Ask Questions Draw a box around two things in the text you would notice when examining rocks closely.

Ask Questions: Extend Your Ideas On a separate sheet of paper, write two questions you might have as you examine a rock.

Make Your Case Underline information in the chart that builds on information in the story.

Make Your Case: Extend Your Ideas On a separate sheet of paper, explain whether the chart is helpful. Use evidence from the text to support your answer.

Students read text closely to determine what the text says.

Name _____

DIRECTIONS Begin planning and prewriting for a news report about the impact of a natural disaster on the Earth and its inhabitants. Brainstorm types of natural disasters and sources you can use to find information about events and effects. Then state your topic, audience, and purpose and gather notes from your research to support your writing. Remember to keep track of each source that you use.

_____

_____

_____

_____

_____

_____

_____

_____

Conventions

Order Adjectives Write the adjectives below in the correct order. Then write your own sentences, ordering adjectives correctly.

1. This round small brown beautiful rock

_____

2. _____

_____

3. _____

_____

Students write routinely for a range of tasks, purposes, and audiences. Students practice various conventions of standard English.

Name _____

DIRECTIONS Use each word in a sentence.

crisis   stranded

_____

_____

_____

**Write in
Response to
Reading**

DIRECTIONS Reread pp. 22–23 of *A Tsunami Unfolds*. Why were crews trying so hard to pump water on the reactors? Use details from the text to support your answer.

_____

_____

_____

_____

Students show contextual understanding of Benchmark Vocabulary. Students write routinely for a range of tasks, purposes, and audiences.

Name _____

DIRECTIONS Draft a news report that informs readers about the effects of a natural disaster on the Earth and its people. Refer to the plan you formed during your prewriting in Lesson 12. Using this plan, you should be able to state your topic and purpose. Then develop the best support, organizing your information into paragraphs, text boxes, visuals, and captions.

_____

_____

_____

_____

_____

_____

_____

Conventions

Prepositional Phrases Write your own sentences using information from *A Tsunami Unfolds*. Remember to include prepositional phrases.

1. _____

_____

2. _____

_____

3. _____

_____

Students write routinely for a range of tasks, purposes, and audiences. Students practice various conventions of standard English.

Name _____

DIRECTIONS Use each word in a sentence.

rescue   mistrusted   grim

_____

_____

_____

_____

_____

Write in Response to Reading

DIRECTIONS Reread pp. 26–29 of *A Tsunami Unfolds*. Write a paragraph that explains the major concerns of radiation contamination. Use details from the text to support your answer.

_____

_____

_____

_____

_____

_____

_____

Students show contextual understanding of Benchmark Vocabulary. Students write routinely for a range of tasks, purposes, and audiences.

Name _____

DIRECTIONS Using evidence from the text, answer the following questions about pp. 26–31 of *A Tsunami Unfolds*.

1. Reread pp. 26–27. What about Japanese victims amazed the world?

   _____

2. Did the Japanese people trust their government's reports on radiation?

   _____

   _____

3. Reread pp. 28–29. What types of illnesses did people experience after the tsunami?

   _____

   _____

4. What did workers use to measure the radiation levels at Daiichi?

   _____

   _____

5. Reread pp. 30–31. What changes have the Japanese people made to prevent another disaster?

   _____

   _____

   _____

Students analyze and respond to literary and informational text.

Name _____

DIRECTIONS Continue writing your news report. Write a conclusion that meets the criteria you have learned. You should aim to present this information in an organized yet creative format. Use one or more headings to group ideas for your conclusion.

_____

_____

_____

_____

_____

_____

_____

Conventions

Prepositional Phrases Circle the preposition. Underline the prepositional object. Then write your own sentences using prepositional phrases.

1. They poured water on the reactor to keep it cool.

2. _____

_____

3. _____

_____

4. _____

_____

Students write routinely for a range of tasks, purposes, and audiences. Students practice various conventions of standard English.

Name _____

Suffixes *-ous, -able, -ible*

Word Bank

famous	flexible	reasonable	fashionable
washable	nervous	various	laughable
convertible	forgettable	humorous	reversible
responsible	divisible	furious	breakable

DIRECTIONS Write the list word that has the same or almost the same meaning as the underlined word or phrase.

1. She wore a <u>stylish</u> new dress.

   1. _____

2. People who are <u>well-known</u> are often stopped by fans on the street.

   2. _____

3. The process was easily <u>able to be changed back</u>.

   3. _____

4. The mayor's proposal was <u>silly</u>.

   4. _____

5. I thought the challenger's proposal was very <u>sensible</u>.

   5. _____

6. I felt <u>worried</u> and had butterflies in my stomach.

   6. _____

7. This shirt is <u>able to be cleaned</u>.

   7. _____

8. The pizza we ordered was evenly <u>divided</u> among us.

   8. _____

DIRECTIONS Write the list word that fits each definition.

9. not easily remembered

   9. _____

10. fragile, easily broken

   10. _____

11. easily changed, car with a folding roof

   11. _____

12. being the primary cause of something

   12. _____

13. full of wild, fierce anger

   13. _____

14. funny and amusing

   14. _____

15. easily bended

   15. _____

16. differing from one another

   16. _____

Students apply grade-level phonics and word analysis skills.

Name _____

DIRECTIONS Use each word in a sentence.

originate   expected   crisis

_____

_____

_____

_____

Write in Response to Reading

DIRECTIONS Revisit *Anatomy of a Volcanic Eruption* and *A Tsunami Unfolds*. How are the structures of the two texts alike? How are they different? Use details from both texts to help explain similarities and differences.

_____

_____

_____

_____

Students show contextual understanding of Benchmark Vocabulary. Students write routinely for a range of tasks, purposes, and audiences.

Name _____

DIRECTIONS Rewrite and revise your news report. Pay special attention to using precise words and phrases. Consult with your sources to locate additional words and information. Remember to only replace words with more exact, or correct words.

_____

_____

_____

_____

_____

_____

_____

_____

_____

_____

_____

Conventions

Progressive Verb Tenses Underline the progressive verb forms in each sentence.

1. The ground will be shaking violently.

2. Waves and tides in oceans are constantly moving sand.

3. Scientists have been finding more and more evidence about how tsunamis are formed.

Students write routinely for a range of tasks, purposes, and audiences. Students practice various conventions of standard English.

Name _____

DIRECTIONS Use each word in a sentence.

interior   pressure   collide   evacuate   survive   anxious

_____

_____

_____

_____

_____

_____

_____

_____

_____

Write in Response to Reading

DIRECTIONS Revisit *Anatomy of a Volcanic Eruption* and *Escape from Pompeii.* Compare how each text presents information about the eruption of Mount Vesuvius. Use details from both texts to support your answer.

_____

_____

_____

_____

_____

Students show contextual understanding of Benchmark Vocabulary. Students write routinely for a range of tasks, purposes, and audiences.

DIRECTIONS Using evidence from the text, answer the following questions about *Anatomy of a Volcanic Eruption, A Tsunami Unfolds*, and *Escape from Pompeii*.

1. Reread pp. 8–9 of *Anatomy of a Volcanic Eruption*. How does the information in this section relate to *A Tsunami Unfolds*?

    _____

    _____

    _____

    _____

2. Reread pp. 12–13 of *A Tsunami Unfolds*. How does the information in this section relate to *Escape from Pompeii*?

    _____

    _____

    _____

    _____

3. Write a paragraph that explores the similarities and differences of each of the three texts. Which text do you think provides the most useful facts and details? Use examples from the texts to support your answer.

    _____

    _____

    _____

    _____

Students analyze and respond to literary and informational text.

Name _____

DIRECTIONS Continue to edit and proofread your news report. Check that you have used proper spelling and correct capitalization. Focus on what you have learned about editing in this lesson to consider the changes you could make to improve your news report.

_____

_____

_____

_____

_____

_____

_____

Conventions

Use Commas Correctly Add a comma or commas to the sentence below. Then write your own sentences, using commas correctly.

1. Livia spent most of her time learning to weave and cook but on hot afternoons she would sit by the fountain.

2. _____

   _____

3. _____

   _____

4. _____

   _____

Students write routinely for a range of tasks, purposes, and audiences. Students practice various conventions of standard English.

Name _____

DIRECTIONS Use each word in a sentence.

investigations   contamination   radiation   desperately

_____

_____

_____

_____

_____

_____

**Write in
Response to
Reading**

DIRECTIONS Do you think current residents of Pompeii should be concerned about a future eruption of Mount Vesuvius? Use details from *Anatomy of a Volcanic Eruption* and *A Tsunami Unfolds* to support your answer.

_____

_____

_____

_____

_____

_____

Students show contextual understanding of Benchmark Vocabulary. Students write routinely for a range of tasks, purposes, and audiences.

Name _____

DIRECTIONS Publish and present your revised and edited news report.
To prepare for your presentation, draft a plan, and rewrite it as necessary.
Then present your news report to the class.

_____

_____

_____

_____

_____

_____

_____

Commas and Quotation Marks Revisit any of the three texts—
Anatomy of a Volcanic Eruption, A Tsunami Unfolds, or *Escape from
Pompeii*. Select three quotations from the text, and reproduce them below.
Remember to use commas correctly.

1. _____

_____

2. _____

_____

3. _____

_____

Students write routinely for a range of
tasks, purposes, and audiences. Students
practice various conventions of standard
English.

Name _____

Related Words

Proofread a Story Help Maggie edit her story about a family member. Circle seven misspelled words. Then write them correctly on the lines below. Use the list of words to help you.

Word Bank
please
pleasant
breath
breathe
image
imagine
product
production
heal
health
triple
triplet
relate
relative
meter
metric
compose
composition
crumb
crumble

A Family Tale

I have a very pleasent and interesting elderly relitive. He is ninety-five years old and is the imige of health. One of his daily healthe habits is to breathe very deeply each morning. Then he starts exercising. Can you imagine someone who's ninety-five doing jumping jacks? I've even seen my relative do this in tripel time. Yesterday he went out and cought a fish that weighed 1,000 pounds. He reeled it in and ate the whole thing for breakfast. Maybe by now you've guessed that this compusition is a tall tale!

1. _____   2. _____

3. _____   4. _____

5. _____   6. _____

7. _____

Proofread Words Circle the word that is spelled correctly.

8. breth   breath   breate

9. health   helth   heathe

10. tiplet   tripplet   triplet

11. crumle   crumble   crumbel

12. metric   metrik   metic

Students apply grade-level phonics and word analysis skills.

Name _____

DIRECTIONS Use each word in a sentence.

amateur   profit   initiative

_____

_____

_____

_____

_____

Write in Response to Reading

DIRECTIONS Reread pp. 1–24 of *Lunch Money*. Do you think Greg is a realistic character? Explain why or why not. Use details from the text to support your answer.

_____

_____

_____

_____

_____

Students show contextual understanding of Benchmark Vocabulary. Students write routinely for a range of tasks, purposes, and audiences.

Name _____

DIRECTIONS Write the beginning of a narrative in which there is a problem that needs to be solved. You will establish a situation by describing the characters or setting and introducing the problem.

_____

_____

_____

_____

_____

_____

_____

_____

Conventions

Order Adjectives Write sentences using multiple adjectives in each sentence. Remember to order your adjectives correctly.

1. _____

_____

2. _____

_____

3. _____

_____

Students write routinely for a range of tasks, purposes, and audiences. Students practice various conventions of standard English.

Name _____

DIRECTIONS Use each word in a sentence.

operation   logically   bargain   accusing

_____

_____

_____

_____

_____

_____

Write in Response to Reading

DIRECTIONS Reread pp. 25–38 of *Lunch Money*. What does the printing and development process of a single Chunky Comic tell you about Greg's character? Use examples and details from the text to support your answer.

_____

_____

_____

_____

Students show contextual understanding of Benchmark Vocabulary. Students write routinely for a range of tasks, purposes, and audiences.

Name _____

DIRECTIONS Using evidence from the text, answer the following
questions about pp. 25–56 of *Lunch Money*.

1. Reread pp. 30–32. What is the purpose of the visuals on these pages?

   _____

   _____

2. How would the story be different if these visuals were removed?

   _____

   _____

3. What do these visuals tell you about Greg's character?

   _____

   _____

4. Reread pp. 37–38. Why do you think the author chose to include the
   cover of The Lost Unicorn?

   _____

   _____

   _____

5. Why does Greg get upset when he sees Maura's comic?

   _____

   _____

   _____

Students analyze and respond to literary and
informational text.

DIRECTIONS Write two or three paragraphs for your narrative about characters who are facing a challenge. Your paragraphs should introduce the narrator and at least one additional character.

_____

_____

_____

_____

_____

_____

_____

_____

_____

_____

Conventions

Pronouns Rewrite the sentences below by replacing nouns with appropriate pronouns.

1. The clash between Greg and Maura had been out in the open.

_____

2. The copier Greg used was Greg's dad's, and it was hooked up to the other computer.

_____

_____

 Students write routinely for a range of tasks, purposes, and audiences. Students practice various conventions of standard English.

Name _____

DIRECTIONS Use each word in a sentence.

chaos   illusion   activate

_____

_____

_____

_____

Write in
Response to
Reading

DIRECTIONS Reread pp. 57–85 of *Lunch Money*. Why is it important for readers to understand how characters feel when they speak? Use evidence from the text to support your answer.

_____

_____

_____

_____

Students show contextual understanding
of Benchmark Vocabulary. Students write
routinely for a range of tasks, purposes, and
audiences.

Name _____

Jesse's Perfect Score

Jesse had no trouble with most of his classes but clearly struggled with science. Just a week ago, Mr. Delgado had suggested that Jesse's parents find him a science tutor. So, when he received an A+ on the astronomy test, Mr. Delgado was pleased—and a little surprised. Then Anton reported that he had seen Jesse looking at his test answers. Mr. Delgado considered Jesse an honest student, but he began wondering whether Jesse had earned that perfect score.

Mr. Delgado was missing important information. First, Jesse had been an astronomy buff for years and was thrilled when the class finally reached that part of science. He had glow-in-the-dark stars on his bedroom ceiling, and photos of planets and galaxies decorated his walls. Second, Jesse had studied especially hard for the test.

Third, Anton was angry at Jesse and wanted revenge. Anton's pride had been wounded. Most days at recess, the other kids chose Jesse for the baseball team before him. Jesse was a better catcher and batter. Anton could not stand it. When Jesse tagged Anton out at home base, Anton promised to make him pay.

Mr. Delgado had to uncover the truth. He began with Jesse. He took him aside, explaining that another student had accused him of cheating on the test. Jesse insisted that he didn't cheat. He was honest and worked hard for his grades. Jesse inquired, "Was the student Anton?"

The surprise on the teacher's face was evident. Jesse explained what happened at recess and described how much he had studied. As he spoke, Jesse gained a new confidence. Mr. Delgado asked questions and listened carefully to Jesse's answers.

He then talked to Anton, who eventually admitted lying, and offered an apology. After thanking Anton for telling the truth, Mr. Delgado discussed the importance of honesty. He emphasized that actions have consequences and told Anton that he owed Jesse an apology. Anton would spend today's recess inside writing that apology.

After Anton finished writing, Mr. Delgado brought the two students together. Jesse listened politely as Anton read the apology aloud. When he

Students read text closely to determine what the text says.

Name _____

finished, Anton asked him nervously if maybe they could be friends—and if maybe they could play on the same team at recess.

"I'd like that," Jesse said.

Gather Evidence Underline the information Mr. Delgado was missing when he wondered whether Jesse cheated on the test.

Gather Evidence: Extend Your Ideas Explain why Mr. Delgado believed Jesse cheated. Would you have come to the same conclusion?

_____

_____

_____

_____

Ask Questions Draw a box around one of the character's reactions. Write a question for that character on why he acted the way he did.

_____

_____

Ask Questions: Extend Your Ideas Write two more questions for another character in the story.

_____

_____

Make Your Case Choose the character you found most interesting and circle the details in the text that describe him.

Make Your Case: Extend Your Ideas On a separate sheet of paper, explain whether that character changed for the better in the story.

Students read text closely to determine what the text says.

Name _____

DIRECTIONS Write a scene of dialogue between two or more characters who work together to come up with creative solutions to a problem. Think about a problem for your narrative. Then, plan the characters and dialogue. Remember to introduce the characters, situation, and problem before you begin writing your dialogue.

_____

_____

_____

_____

_____

_____

_____

_____

Relative Pronouns Circle the relative pronouns. Then underline the noun each describes.

1. He had piercing dark eyes and a bright smile, which made it harder to notice the large nose that lived between them.

2. Greg squinted at the comic in his hand, which wasn't his own and bothered him.

3. Numbers never bleed, which Mr. Z believed was one of their best qualities.

4. Greg smiled, which forced a sharp pain up through his nose.

Students write routinely for a range of tasks, purposes, and audiences. Students practice various conventions of standard English.

Name _____

DIRECTIONS Use each word in a sentence.

irrational   production   imitation

_____

_____

_____

_____

> **Write in Response to Reading**

DIRECTIONS Reread pp. 97–99 of *Lunch Money*. Is Greg's embarrassment a result of only having a black eye, or is it more from the fact that a girl gave him the black eye? Use evidence from the text to support your answer.

_____

_____

_____

_____

_____

_____

Students show contextual understanding of Benchmark Vocabulary. Students write routinely for a range of tasks, purposes, and audiences.

Name _____

DIRECTIONS Using evidence from the text, answer the following questions about pp. 86–109 of *Lunch Money*.

1. On p. 89, Mr. Z says that Greg and Maura can't be friends because they are too much alike. In what ways are they alike?

   _____

   _____

2. Draw an inference about why it might be hard for Greg and Maura to be friends.

   _____

   _____

   _____

3. On p. 93, Greg asks why Mr. Z's brother lives in Idaho rather than in Chicago or Florida. Draw an inference about why Greg asked that question.

   _____

   _____

4. Why does Mr. Z tell Greg: "Most people can only use one bathroom at a time"? Make an inference based on what you have read about Mr. Z so far.

   _____

   _____

   _____

Students analyze and respond to literary and informational text.

Name _____

DIRECTIONS Write the opening paragraph of a narrative in which a character or third-person narrator describes the setting of the story. Your writing should be from the point of view of the narrator and include concrete words and phrases that precisely convey details of the setting and events.

_____

_____

_____

_____

_____

_____

Conventions

Subject-Verb Agreement Correct subject-verb agreement by rewriting the sentences below. Then write your own sentence using correct subject-verb agreement.

1. So, Mr. Z, do you wishes sometimes that you could have been a doctor?

_____

_____

2. Greg wish that he hadn't received a black eye!

_____

_____

3. _____

_____

Students write routinely for a range of tasks, purposes, and audiences. Students practice various conventions of standard English.

Name _____

DIRECTIONS Use each word in a sentence.

empire   conceited

_____

_____

_____

_____

**Write in
Response to
Reading**

DIRECTIONS Revisit Chapters 12–14 of *Lunch Money*. What effect do
you think Maura will have on Greg's business? Use evidence from the
text to summarize how you believe Maura will help or harm Greg's comic
book business.

_____

_____

_____

_____

Students show contextual understanding
of Benchmark Vocabulary. Students write
routinely for a range of tasks, purposes,
and audiences.

Name _____

DIRECTIONS Imagine a story that is set at a small business. Research details about the business that you can use to help you describe the setting. Write a few opening paragraphs that introduce either your narrator or a character. Remember to use authentic details from your research to help you describe the setting.

_____

_____

_____

_____

_____

_____

_____

Conventions

Pronoun-Antecedent Agreement Circle the pronoun, and underline its antecedent. Then write two of your own sentences. Remember to circle the pronoun and underline its antecedent.

1. There was a close-up of the unicorn's head with its teeth showing and nostrils snorting.

2. _____

_____

3. _____

_____

Students write routinely for a range of tasks, purposes, and audiences. Students practice various conventions of standard English.

Suffix *–ion*

Word Bank			
justification	pollution	suggestion	quotation
correction	proclamation	audition	publication
improvisation	transition	altercation	election

DIRECTIONS Complete each sentence with a list word.

1. Every four years, there is an _____ to select the next president.

1. _____

2. Recycling is one way to reduce _____.

2. _____

3. My teacher wanted me to add another _____ to my paper.

3. _____

4. I'm planning to _____ for the school play.

4. _____

5. What's your _____ for spending so much money? 5. _____

6. Abraham Lincoln signed the Emancipation _____. 6. _____

7. It's better to avoid an _____ and talk things out. 7. _____

8. To my recollection, my homework had only one _____.

8. _____

9. Chris just moved here, and the _____ is difficult for him.

9. _____

10. He asked me a question, so I made a _____. 10. _____

DIRECTIONS Choose two words from the above list, and write a sentence for each word.

11. _____

_____

12. _____

_____

Students apply grade-level phonics and word analysis skills.

Name _____

DIRECTIONS Use each word in a sentence.

contrast   contritely

_____

_____

_____

Write in Response to Reading

DIRECTIONS Reread pp. 139–150 of *Lunch Money*. What is the most important element of a great comic book? Use details and evidence from the text to support your opinion.

_____

_____

_____

_____

_____

Students show contextual understanding of Benchmark Vocabulary. Students write routinely for a range of tasks, purposes, and audiences.

Writing

Name _____

DIRECTIONS Write a scene about two or more characters who are working together to solve a problem. Remember to include descriptive details.

_____

_____

_____

_____

_____

_____

_____

Conventions

Use Adverbs Circle the adverb in the sentence below. Write a synonym for that adverb on the line. Then write two of your own sentences using adverbs.

1. Because what she saw reminded her of two kindergartners at the art tables, each child bent over some work, each completely unaware of the other.

_____

2. _____

_____

3. _____

_____

Students write routinely for a range of tasks, purposes, and audiences. Students practice various conventions of standard English.

Name _____

DIRECTIONS Use each word in a sentence.

efficient   derailed   controversy

_____

_____

_____

_____

Write in Response to Reading

DIRECTIONS Reread pp. 164–182 of *Lunch Money*. Write a character analysis of Mrs. Davenport. Use specific details and evidence from the text to support your answer.

_____

_____

_____

_____

_____

Students show contextual understanding of Benchmark Vocabulary. Students write routinely for a range of tasks, purposes, and audiences.

Name _____

DIRECTIONS Using evidence from the text, answer the following questions about pp. 164–182 of *Lunch Money*.

1. Reread the second paragraph on p. 167. What do you learn about Maura's character from this paragraph?

   _____

   _____

   _____

2. Reread the first two paragraphs on p. 169. What do you learn about Greg's character from these paragraphs?

   _____

   _____

   _____

3. Reread pp. 171–176. What do you learn about Mr. Z's character in this section? Include at least two direct quotations from the text to support your answer.

   _____

   _____

   _____

4. Summarize your favorite character. What character traits do they possess that you admire? Use details from the text to support your answer.

   _____

   _____

   _____

Students analyze and respond to literary and informational text.

Name _____

DIRECTIONS Write about your actions, thoughts, or feelings from an experience you had that involved making a big decision. Organize your information as a sequence of events. Remember to use transitional words.

_____

_____

_____

_____

_____

_____

_____

Conventions

Prepositional Phrases Underline the prepositional phrases in the sentences below. Then write two of your own sentences using prepositional phrases.

1. She slipped it inside the front cover of her social studies book and then they both ran and got on the bus.

2. Mr. Z pulled a handful of papers from the in-box on his desk.

3. _____

_____

4. _____

_____

 Students write routinely for a range of tasks, purposes, and audiences. Students practice various conventions of standard English.

Name _____

DIRECTIONS Use each word in a sentence.

agenda   pioneering

_____

_____

_____

Write in Response to Reading

DIRECTIONS Reread the second paragraph on p. 189 of *Lunch Money*. What descriptive words does the author use to describe Mrs. Chalmers? What do these words tell you about her character? Use examples from the text to support your answer.

_____

_____

_____

_____

_____

_____

Students show contextual understanding of Benchmark Vocabulary. Students write routinely for a range of tasks, purposes, and audiences.

Name _____

DIRECTIONS Write a draft of a narrative about two characters competing to sell similar products. Use sensory details to convey events precisely, make the narrative more vivid, and to develop your theme.

_____

_____

_____

_____

_____

_____

_____

Progressive Verb Tenses Write your own sentences using progressive verb tenses.

1. _____

_____

2. _____

_____

3. _____

_____

Students write routinely for a range of tasks, purposes, and audiences. Students practice various conventions of standard English.

Name _____

DIRECTIONS Use each word in a sentence.

confession   privilege   negotiations

_____

_____

_____

_____

_____

Write in Response to Reading

DIRECTIONS Reread pp. 203–222 of *Lunch Money*. What do you think is the most important theme in *Lunch Money?* Identify the theme, record story details that support the theme, and then explain why it's important to Greg's character development. Use examples from the text to support your answer.

_____

_____

_____

_____

_____

_____

_____

Students show contextual understanding of Benchmark Vocabulary. Students write routinely for a range of tasks, purposes, and audiences.

Name _____

DIRECTIONS Using evidence from the text, answer the following questions about pp. 203–222 from *Lunch Money*.

1. One theme in the story is standing up for what you believe in. How do the students' actions support this theme?

_____

_____

_____

2. What does Greg realize at the end of Chapter 23? How does his realization support the theme of standing up for what you believe in?

_____

_____

_____

3. Select one of the characters in the book. Do you think he or she learns this lesson? Explain your response using evidence from the text.

_____

_____

_____

4. Does the act of sending the comic books anonymously to Mrs. Davenport support or go against this theme? Explain your response using evidence from the text.

_____

_____

_____

Students analyze and respond to literary and informational text.

Writing

Name _____

DIRECTIONS Write a sequel to *Lunch Money* in which Greg and Maura discuss adding a new product to their Chunky Comics business. Use dialogue to reveal what each character thinks the new product should be. Remember to include a conclusion that logically follows earlier events.

_____

_____

_____

_____

_____

_____

_____

_____

Conventions

Coordinating Conjunctions Write a coordinating conjunction to complete the sentences below. Then write two of your own sentences using coordinating conjunctions.

1. Maura studied books from the library _____ practiced hard to learn how to draw a comic book.

2. Greg started to follow, _____ then he stopped.

3. _____

   _____

4. _____

   _____

Students write routinely for a range of tasks, purposes, and audiences. Students practice various conventions of standard English.

Name _____

DIRECTIONS Use each word in a sentence.

victory   fortune

_____

_____

_____

**Write in
Response to
Reading**

DIRECTIONS Reread pp. 74–80 of *Max Malone Makes a Million*. Tell how the author introduces a main idea and supports it with characters' actions, words, and thoughts. Then explain how this strategy helps readers connect with Max. Use details from the text to support your answer.

_____

_____

_____

_____

_____

_____

Students show contextual understanding of Benchmark Vocabulary. Students write routinely for a range of tasks, purposes, and audiences.

Name _____

DIRECTIONS Write a narrative about what you would do with your profits if you operated a million-dollar business. You should establish the business situation of your narrative by having your narrator do something, think about something, or report it with pieces of dialogue. Then introduce your characters, setting, and plot events. Remember to use transitional words and phrases to manage your narrative's sequence of events.

_____

_____

_____

_____

_____

_____

Conventions

Modal Auxiliaries Underline the modal auxiliary in the following sentences. Then write two of your own sentences that describe Max Malone. Remember to use modal auxiliaries.

1. This young man may be well on his way to becoming a millionaire.

2. They could sell frozen lemonade in a supermarket.

3. _____

_____

4. _____

_____

Students write routinely for a range of tasks, purposes, and audiences. Students practice various conventions of standard English.

Name _____

Words from German

Word Bank

bagel	knapsack	hamster	waltz
glitz	gestalt	angst	pretzel
seltzer	nosh	bratwurst	noodle

DIRECTIONS Write a list word for each description. Use a dictionary to help you.

1. backpack made of canvas

    1. _____

2. perceived as more than the sum of its parts

    2. _____

3. German pork sausage

    3. _____

4. extravagant, glamorous, or superficial

    4. _____

5. small rodent

    5. _____

6. crisp bread that is baked and salty

    6. _____

7. to eat a bit of food or a snack

    7. _____

8. strip, ring, or tube of pasta often made with egg

    8. _____

9. carbonated water

    9. _____

10. partner dance that means "to turn" in German

    10. _____

11. a deep anxiety, or fear

    11. _____

12. doughy bread shaped like a ring

    12. _____

Students apply grade-level phonics and word analysis skills.

Name _____

DIRECTIONS Use each word in a sentence.

enveloped   quality

_____

_____

_____

DIRECTIONS Reread pp. 81–87 of *Max Malone Makes a Million*. Do you think baking and selling cookies is a good plan to make a million dollars? Use examples and details from the text in sequential order to support your ideas.

_____

_____

_____

_____

_____

Students show contextual understanding of Benchmark Vocabulary. Students write routinely for a range of tasks, purposes, and audiences.

Name _____

DIRECTIONS Write a conclusion to the story that tells what happens next for Max and Gordy. You may choose any type of event for the characters, but your conclusion should follow logically from the events that you have read so far. Remember to revise your writing to make sure it is clear and on topic.

_____

_____

_____

_____

_____

_____

Conventions

Commas and Quotation Marks in Dialogue Punctuate the sentences below, using commas and quotation marks correctly. Then write one sentence of your own dialogue. Remember to use commas and quotation marks properly.

1. Check answered Max.

2. I think I'd better leave said Mrs. Malone touching her hand to her forehead and hurrying out of the kitchen.

3. Austin is selling lemonade said Max.

4. _____

_____

Students write routinely for a range of tasks, purposes, and audiences. Students practice various conventions of standard English.

Name _____

DIRECTIONS Use the word below in a sentence.

insulted

_____

_____

**Write in
Response to
Reading**

DIRECTIONS Reread pp. 88–93 of *Max Malone Makes a Million*.
Would you want to compete with a friend to sell lemonade? Explain why
or why not. Use careful word choice to describe how competing with a
friend would make you feel. Use examples and evidence from the text to
support your answer.

_____

_____

_____

_____

_____

_____

_____

Students show contextual understanding
of Benchmark Vocabulary. Students write
routinely for a range of tasks, purposes,
and audiences.

Name _____

DIRECTIONS Using evidence from the text, answer the following questions about pp. 88–93 from *Max Malone Makes a Million.*

1. Reread the fifth paragraph on p. 88. What is the mood of this paragraph?

   _____

   _____

2. What specific words does the author choose to include that help create the mood?

   _____

   _____

3. Reread the first four paragraphs on p. 89. How does the mood in these early paragraphs change from the previous page?

   _____

   _____

4. What specific words does the author choose to include that help change the mood?

   _____

   _____

5. Reread p. 93. What mood does the author create at the end of the story? Do you think the mood is appropriate? Use details from the text to support your answer.

   _____

   _____

Students analyze and respond to literary and informational text.

Name _____

DIRECTIONS Write a narrative about a solution to a specific problem. Include decisions that characters have to make in order to work together and solve the problem.

_____

_____

_____

_____

_____

_____

_____

_____

_____

_____

Conventions

Produce Complete Sentences Rewrite the fragments below as complete sentences. Then write your own complete sentence about Max. Use information from pp. 88–93 of *Max Malone Makes a Million* to help you.

1. One thing I love about school.

_____

_____

2. will sell lemonade

_____

_____

3. _____

_____

Students write routinely for a range of tasks, purposes, and audiences. Students practice various conventions of standard English.

Name _____

DIRECTIONS Use each word in a sentence.

amateur   profit   initiative   victory   fortune

_____

_____

_____

_____

_____

_____

Write in Response to Reading

DIRECTIONS Revisit *Lunch Money* and *Max Malone Makes a Million*. Which character do you think had the most creative ideas about making money--Greg or Max? Use specific examples from both texts to support your answer.

_____

_____

_____

_____

_____

_____

_____

_____

Students show contextual understanding of Benchmark Vocabulary. Students write routinely for a range of tasks, purposes, and audiences.

Team "Sports"

Alec and Joey lived near the ocean all year long. Most people don't realize how boring and lonely winter can be at the beach, especially when you and your brother like doing different things. The summer, though, was an entirely different story.

The beach was bustling every week as vacationers came and went. An outgoing boy, Alec—the older by two years—was famous for organizing games of beach volleyball, football, and any other sport imaginable. Sometimes Joey, who was on the shy side, tried to join in. But often he preferred to draw, paint, or build fancy sandcastles like his grandmother. She had taught him how to pack the sand tightly with his palms, carving rounded windows and delicate towers with a garden spade.

Alec didn't understand why Joey would rather do artistic things than play ball. When Joey tried to explain, Alec just shook his head. He insisted that sports were better because sports often allowed many kids to play together. That is when Joey's idea hatched. He would show Alec what doing things together looked like!

Working for several hours, Joey created an elaborate sandcastle with stairs, towers, and shell-lined walls. When he had finished, he used his mom's camera to take pictures. Then Joey painted colorful posters featuring his sandcastle and the question, "Can you top this?" He hung his posters everywhere in town, announcing his plans for a day of sandcastle artistry—all ages welcome. At the end of the day, there would be a potluck dinner to mark the occasion.

When Alec saw a poster, he smirked and not so nicely told Joey that no one would come. Still, shortly after sunrise on Saturday, Joey was on the beach digging in the sand. By midmorning, four kids his age were sculpting the sand alongside him. By noon the number had tripled. A couple of parents even joined in. Joey beamed as everyone eagerly discussed ideas and shared tools. It was a sandcastle-making party!

As the afternoon progressed, Alec's game of volleyball died down, and his friends suggested they check out the sand structures. Alec couldn't believe what he saw. At least 30 people were building an entire city of sandcastles! It was one of the most beautiful things he had seen on the beach. Best yet, everyone was chatting and laughing and working together.

Students read text closely to determine what the text says.

Name _____

"Well, little brother," Alec said to Joey, "I guess you proved me wrong. You should make this sandcastle day an annual tradition!" With a chuckle, Joey handed Alec and his buddies a pail and several shovels and told them to get started on their own castle masterpieces. Before long, they too were working together on a super creation in the sand.

Gather Evidence Underline two details about Alec, and two about Joey.

Gather Evidence: Extend Your Ideas What are some differences between Alec and Joey?

_____

Ask Questions Write two questions about the characters that would help you better understand them.

_____

_____

Ask Questions: Extend Your Ideas On a separate sheet of paper, write three other questions about Alec and Joey that interest you.

Make Your Case Circle clues in the text that show how Alec and Joey change from the beginning to the end of the story.

Make Your Case: Extend Your Ideas Who changed more from the beginning to the end of the story: Alec or Joey? On a separate sheet of paper, explain your answer using details from the text to identify the specific change(s).

Students read text closely to determine what the text says.

Name _____

DIRECTIONS Complete your Story Sequence charts. Then write a preliminary draft of a narrative about a main character and what he or she might discover that changes his or her life. Remember that your events should follow a sequence that unfolds naturally.

_____

_____

_____

_____

_____

_____

_____

Combine Sentences Combine the sentence below using a comma and a coordinating conjunction. Then write two of your own sentences. Remember to include a comma and coordinating conjunction.

1. At first my aunt was surprised and happy to see us. Then Chaco told her why we were there.

_____

_____

2. _____

_____

3. _____

_____

Students write routinely for a range of tasks, purposes, and audiences. Students practice various conventions of standard English.

Name _____

DIRECTIONS Use the word below in a sentence.

inspection

_____

_____

Write in Response to Reading

DIRECTIONS Reread pp. 58–66 of *Coyote School News.* How is Monchi's hometown different from Tucson? Use specific details and evidence from the text to support your answer.

_____

_____

_____

_____

_____

_____

_____

Students show contextual understanding of Benchmark Vocabulary. Students write routinely for a range of tasks, purposes, and audiences.

Name _____

DIRECTIONS Review your prewriting notes. Then begin drafting your narrative about a character who makes a discovery that changes his or her life. Focus on getting all of your ideas on paper to flesh out your story. You will have another opportunity to revise. After you have finished your draft, reread it to ensure that it is well organized and clear. Add transitional words or phrases to better connect ideas.

_____

_____

_____

_____

_____

_____

_____

_____

Conventions

Relative Adverbs Circle the relative adverb in the sentences below.

1. Chaco drove us to school where Miss Byers was our teacher.

2. I like Rosie, but I hate it when Natalia teases me.

3. At first my aunt was surprised and happy to see us, but then my tío told her why we were there.

4. I didn't want to look when she gave him the silver dollar.

Students write routinely for a range of tasks, purposes, and audiences. Students practice various conventions of standard English.

Name _____

DIRECTIONS Use each word in a sentence.

promoted   contributed

_____

_____

_____

**Write in
Response to
Reading**

DIRECTIONS Reread pp. 67–73 of *Coyote School News*. Would you
want to attend a school that's similar to Coyote School? Does your answer
connect with the theme of the text? Explain why or why not. Use specific
details and examples from the text to support your answer.

_____

_____

_____

_____

_____

_____

_____

Students show contextual understanding
of Benchmark Vocabulary. Students write
routinely for a range of tasks, purposes, and
audiences.

Name _____

DIRECTIONS Using evidence from the text, answer the following questions about pp. 67–73 from *Coyote School News*.

1. How can you tell that a word in the text is in Spanish?

   _____

   _____

2. From what you read on p. 67, is *Nochebuena* a special day? How do you know?

   _____

   _____

   _____

3. What can you tell about what a *piñata* is from reading only the text on p. 67?

   _____

   _____

4. What can you tell about what *dulces* are from reading only the text on p. 67?

   _____

   _____

5. Why is *novia* not called out in the text on p. 71?

   _____

   _____

   _____

   _____

Students analyze and respond to literary and informational text.

Name _____

DIRECTIONS Write a conclusion to the narrative you have been working on. Review the events of your narrative and consider its message or theme. Use this information to help you write your conclusion.

_____

_____

_____

_____

Conventions

Complex Sentences Underline the dependent clause in the sentence below. Then write three of your own complex sentences using details from pp. 67–73 of *Coyote School News*.

1. When she gave him the silver dollar, I didn't want to look.

2. _____

   _____

3. _____

   _____

4. _____

   _____

Students write routinely for a range of tasks, purposes, and audiences. Students practice various conventions of standard English.

Homographs

Word Bank

tear	fine	wind	bat
desert	object	produce	wound
change	digest	foot	lead

DIRECTIONS Read each sentence. Circle the correct definition for the underlined word.

1. Susan noticed a <u>bat</u> flying in the sky.

    (a piece of sporting equipment / a winged animal)

2. I didn't mean to <u>tear</u> a page out of my notebook!

    (to rip / a drop of water from the eye)

3. I <u>object</u> to the way I'm being treated.

    (a thing / to be opposed to / a goal)

4. It's always cold in the <u>produce</u> section of the supermarket.

    (to create or make / fresh fruits or vegetables)

DIRECTIONS Write a list word to complete each sentence. Then write a definition for the word.

5. The class will learn about the _____ environment next week.

6. If a person drives too fast, then he or she might receive a _____.

7. The _____ was blowing leaves around the courtyard.

8. The doctor told Jackie's mom that her _____ was healing nicely.

9. I received my _____ from the cashier.

10. My brother published a _____ of his findings.

11. I broke my _____ playing basketball.

12. The coach told me it was my turn to _____ the team drill.

Students apply grade-level phonics and word analysis skills.

Benchmark Vocabulary

Name _____

DIRECTIONS Use each word in a sentence.

irrational   production   imitation   inspection

_____

_____

_____

_____

_____

_____

Write in Response to Reading

DIRECTIONS Revisit *Lunch Money* and *Coyote School News*. What do you think motivates Greg to create comic books? What motivates Monchi to work on the school newspaper? Are their motivations similar? Use details from both texts to support your answer.

_____

_____

_____

_____

_____

_____

_____

Students show contextual understanding of Benchmark Vocabulary. Students write routinely for a range of tasks, purposes, and audiences.

Name _____

DIRECTIONS Reread the draft of your narrative. Revise the beginning to ensure that you have established a clear situation, introduced the narrator, and provided details about the setting. Include additional dialogue and sensory details wherever possible. Then make sure that your conclusion follows logically from the events that came before.

_____

_____

_____

_____

_____

_____

_____

_____

Conventions

Compound Sentences Write two of your own sentences using coordinating conjunctions.

1. _____

_____

2. _____

_____

Students write routinely for a range of tasks, purposes, and audiences.
Students practice various conventions of standard English.

Name _____

DIRECTIONS Use each word in a sentence.

efficient   derailed   controversy   promoted   enveloped   quality

_____

_____

_____

_____

_____

_____

_____

Write in Response to Reading

DIRECTIONS Revisit *Lunch Money, Max Malone Makes a Million*, and *Coyote School News*. Write a compare and contrast paragraph about two characters you have read about. You must choose two characters from **different** texts. Use specific details and examples from both texts to support your answer.

_____

_____

_____

_____

_____

_____

Students show contextual understanding of Benchmark Vocabulary. Students write routinely for a range of tasks, purposes, and audiences.

Name _____

DIRECTIONS Using evidence from the text, answer the following
questions about *Lunch Money* and *Max Malone Makes a Million*.

1. How is *Lunch Money* structured?

   _____

2. How is *Max Malone Makes a Million* structured?

   _____

3. What visual elements do both texts have?

   _____

4. Name one visual element that is different in the texts.

   _____

   _____

   _____

5. How did the authors of *Lunch Money* and *Max Malone Makes a
   Million* organize their stories similarly?

   _____

   _____

   _____

   _____

6. Why do you think the authors chose to organize their stories this
   way? Use evidence from the texts to support your answer.

   _____

   _____

   _____

Students analyze and respond to literary
and informational text.

Name _____

DIRECTIONS Edit and proofread the story you wrote in Lesson 13. Make sure that you have used correct spelling and grammar. Check that you have used proper punctuation for dialogue and contractions. Then, verify that you have used a variety of sentence structures.

_____

_____

_____

_____

_____

_____

_____

_____

_____

Conventions

Compound Sentences Circle the coordinating conjunction that needs a comma before it.

1. It was very exciting but now it is over.

2. He saw her shoulders stiffen so he talked fast and kept his voice low.

3. Rosalie could eat tons of sugared cereal and she would never get tired of it.

4. So I got a cast of plaster on my arm and I had to stay in Tucson.

Students write routinely for a range of tasks, purposes, and audiences. Students practice various conventions of standard English.

DIRECTIONS Use each word in a sentence.

confession   privilege   negotiations   contributed   insulted

_____

_____

_____

_____

_____

_____

_____

**Write in
Response to
Reading**

DIRECTIONS Revisit *Lunch Money* and "Coyote School News." Aside from the setting, in what ways are the events of these texts similar? Use details from both texts to support your answer.

_____

_____

_____

_____

_____

_____

Students show contextual understanding of Benchmark Vocabulary. Students write routinely for a range of tasks, purposes, and audiences.

DIRECTIONS Publish and present the story you began in Lesson 13.
Draft a plan for your presentation, altering your writing as necessary.
Write the plan for your presentation on the lines below. Then present your
writing to the class.

_____

_____

_____

_____

_____

_____

_____

_____

Conventions

Spell Grade-Appropriate Words Correctly Circle the misspelled words.
Then write the correct spelling of the words.

1. The school comitee meets tonight in the munisipal building.

_____

2. They pored themselves some moor lemonade.

_____

3. The best was a silver buckel with a whole to put a silver dollar.

_____

Students write routinely for a range of tasks,
purposes, and audiences. Students practice
various conventions of standard English.

Name _____

Latin Roots *gener, port*

Word Bank

general	reporter	portable	support	genius
porter	genes	transported	genealogy	export
generalize	import	generates	port	generous

Words in Context Write a list word to complete each sentence. Use a dictionary or thesaurus to help you.

1. The place where ships unload goods is called a _____. 1. _____

2. My friend's mom is the _____ manager of the hardware store. 2. _____

3. Albert Einstein was a _____ at physics. 3. _____

4. A person whose job requires him or her to carry bags is called a _____. 4. _____

5. She started a business to _____ goods to Italy. 5. _____

6. _____ is the study of one's family lineage. 6. _____

7. To _____ is to speak broadly about a topic. 7. _____

8. My uncle wants to _____ a new car from India. 8. _____

9. The local news _____ was talking about the historic snowstorm. 9. _____

10. Parents pass along their _____ to offspring. 10. _____

11. I will _____ any decision you make. 11. _____

12. This machine _____ electricity. 12. _____

13. I _____ fresh tomatoes from the garden to my home. 13. _____

14. My grandma is a very _____ person. 14. _____

15. I prefer smaller phones because they are more _____. 15. _____

Students apply grade-level phonics and word analysis skills.

Name _____

DIRECTIONS Use each word in a sentence.

value   allowance

_____

_____

_____

_____

Write in Response to Reading

DIRECTIONS Reread pp. 4–7 of *Using Money*. How is using money different from bartering? Use reasons and evidence from the text to support your answer.

_____

_____

_____

_____

_____

_____

_____

_____

Students show contextual understanding of Benchmark Vocabulary. Students write routinely for a range of tasks, purposes, and audiences.

Lesson 1

Name _____

DIRECTIONS Using evidence from the text, answer the following questions about pp. 4–7 of *Using Money*.

1. What is the genre of this text?

_____

2. How can you tell the genre of a text?

_____

_____

_____

3. Reread pp. 6–7. What is the main idea of this section?

_____

_____

_____

4. List three details from this section that support the main idea.

_____

_____

_____

5. What are some things that you can do with your money?

_____

_____

_____

Students analyze and respond to literary and informational text.

DIRECTIONS Write a paragraph about which money system you think is better—the modern money system or the ancient bartering system. Use reasons and evidence from pp. 4–5 of *Using Money* to support your opinion.

_____

_____

_____

_____

_____

_____

Conventions

Relative Pronouns Underline the relative pronoun. Circle the noun that is described by the relative clause. Then write two of your own sentences about money using relative pronouns.

1. A paycheck, which is money earned on a job, is something people receive.

2. People who want to get rid of their old things could have a garage sale.

3. _____

_____

4. _____

_____

Students write routinely for a range of tasks, purposes, and audiences. Students practice various conventions of standard English.

Latin Roots *dur, ject*

Word Bank

adjacent	dejected	procedure	trajectory	objection
endure	obdurate	injection	duration	duress
durable	reject	abject	eject	project

Word Definitions Write the list word that has the same meaning. Use a dictionary or thesaurus to help you.

1. a strong feeling of disapproval or protest 　　1. _____

2. refusing to change one's opinion, stubborn 　　2. _____

3. strong, able to last a long time 　　3. _____

4. to throw, or move something forward 　　4. _____

5. a way of administering a vaccine 　　5. _____

6. able to tolerate that which is unpleasant 　　6. _____

7. threats or actions to make someone do something 　　7. _____

8. to force or throw something out 　　8. _____

9. extremely bad or unbearable 　　9. _____

10. to dismiss 　　10. _____

11. sad, depressed, unhappy 　　11. _____

12. next to something 　　12. _____

13. the length of something 　　13. _____

14. process, steps to complete a task 　　14. _____

15. the path of something 　　15. _____

Students apply grade-level phonics and word analysis skills.

Name _____

DIRECTIONS Use each word in a sentence.

service   charges

_____

_____

_____

DIRECTIONS Reread pp. 8–15 of *Using Money*. Do you think that banks should require a parent's name on an account for children? Use reasons and evidence from the text to support your opinion.

_____

_____

_____

_____

_____

_____

_____

_____

Students show contextual understanding of Benchmark Vocabulary. Students write routinely for a range of tasks, purposes, and audiences.

Name _____

DIRECTIONS Write an opinion paragraph telling whether you think it is important to save money. Use at least two details from pp. 8–15 of *Using Money* to support your opinion. You should also include at least one direct quotation from the text. Remember to use linking words and phrases to connect your reasons and evidence.

_____

_____

_____

_____

_____

_____

_____

Conventions

Commas and Quotation Marks Use commas and quotation marks to punctuate the sentence correctly. Then write three of your own sentences using quotations from *Using Money*.

1. In *Using Money,* the writer says   Saving money is not easy, but the benefits are worth it.

2. _____

   _____

3. _____

   _____

4. _____

   _____

Students write routinely for a range of tasks, purposes, and audiences. Students practice various conventions of standard English.

Name _____

DIRECTIONS Use each word in a sentence.

current   convenience   security

_____

_____

_____

_____

DIRECTIONS Reread pp. 16–21 of *Using Money*. How are the terms *PIN, EFT,* and *ATM* used when discussing the topic of banking? Use evidence from the text to support your answer.

_____

_____

_____

_____

Students show contextual understanding of Benchmark Vocabulary. Students write routinely for a range of tasks, purposes, and audiences.

Name _____

To Save or to Spend?

You just returned from the mall with your friends. You stopped at your favorite store and picked out the next thing you want to buy. All your friends spent their money on little things like fake dinosaur bones, crystals that grow, and a question and answer book about space. Everyone was excited about what they bought and couldn't wait to get home to play with what they picked out.

You, on the other hand, loved a cool rover model and are thinking about saving the money you earned from doing chores to buy it. You have $25.00 but you need to save $50.00 to get it. You also saw a model of a motor, and it was only $25.00. It looked pretty cool. The model teaches you all about an engine and how it works. Cars, airplanes, and even space rovers depend on engines, so it would be cool to learn how one works.

Now you have a dilemma. How should you spend your hard-earned money? In order to solve this problem, you have to look at both options. If you spend the money on the motor model, you'll have something new to play with right away. You can learn all about how an engine works. Then again, the rover model was very cool! It's expensive, and you'd have to save up for it, but there are over 40 different experiments you could do with it.

So now it's decision time! If you wait to get the rover model, you'll have to give up buying the motor model today.

On the other hand, suppose you spend the money on the motor model. What happens when you learn about how an engine works? There aren't 40 different experiments to do with the motor model. Would your choice be a good one, or would you wish you'd saved your money and spent it on the cool rover model instead?

Life is full of decisions and choices. Many have to do with money and things. So keep this proverb in mind, "The art is not in making money, but in keeping it." Remember that your hard-earned money should be spent wisely, and sometimes the wisest thing is not to spend it all.

Students read text closely to determine what the text says.

Name _____

Gather Evidence Underline the options in the text. Use text evidence to explain why it may be beneficial to buy the model of the motor.

_____

_____

Gather Evidence: Extend Your Ideas How would you choose? Use text evidence to explain your choice.

_____

Ask Questions What three questions would you have for the toymakers about each model?

_____

_____

_____

_____

Ask Questions: Extend Your Ideas Suppose you decide on the rover model. What are two additional questions you might have?

_____

Make Your Case Is the author taking a side or remaining neutral about spending habits? Circle the evidence and then explain it in your own words.

_____

_____

Make Your Case: Extend Your Ideas Based on the evidence you circled, state whether you agree or disagree with the author.

_____

_____

Students read text closely to determine what the text says.

Name _____

DIRECTIONS Which do you think is more useful—traditional banking or online banking? Reread pp. 16–21 of *Using Money,* and use the information from this section to form your opinion. Then write an opinion statement that is supported by facts and details from the text. Remember to use linking words and phrases to connect your ideas.

_____

_____

_____

_____

_____

_____

Conventions

Relative Adverbs Circle the relative adverbs in the sentences below. Then write two of your own sentences using relative adverbs.

1. Your check register is where you must record all payments, withdrawals, and deposits.

2. When you have enough money saved, you may deposit it in a savings account.

3. _____

_____

4. _____

_____

Students write routinely for a range of tasks, purposes, and audiences. Students practice various conventions of standard English.

Name _____

DIRECTIONS Use each word in a sentence.

options   cancel

_____

_____

_____

_____

**Write in
Response to
Reading**

DIRECTIONS Reread pp. 22–29 of *Using Money*. Do you think children should be allowed to have credit cards of their own? Use reasons and evidence from the text to support your answer.

_____

_____

_____

_____

_____

_____

_____

Students show contextual understanding
of Benchmark Vocabulary. Students write
routinely for a range of tasks, purposes, and
audiences.

Lesson 4

Name _____

Reading Analysis

DIRECTIONS Using evidence from the text, answer the following questions about pp. 22–29 of *Using Money.*

1. What is interest?

   _____

   _____

2. Will you pay more if you only pay the minimum payment due on a credit card bill?

   _____

   _____

   _____

3. If you pay off most of the credit card bill, will you still need to pay interest?

   _____

   _____

4. What might happen if someone "maxed out" his or her credit card?

   _____

   _____

5. Draw a conclusion to explain why someone might not get a loan if he or she has bad credit.

   _____

6. Draw a conclusion to explain how a person with bad credit could improve his or her credit.

   _____

   _____

Students analyze and respond to literary and informational text.

Name _____

DIRECTIONS Create an informational brochure about a new kind of credit card that will benefit people. Give the credit card a name, and provide reasons why it would help people. Remember to present your writing in the form of a brochure and to include your opinion about the new credit card. Support your opinion with strong reasons and evidence.

_____

_____

_____

_____

_____

_____

Progressive Verb Tenses Change the sentence to both the past and future progressive. Then write two of your own sentences—one in the past progressive and one in the future progressive.

1. The bank is charging a fee.

   past progressive: _____

   future progressive: _____

2. _____

   _____

3. _____

   _____

Students write routinely for a range of tasks, purposes, and audiences. Students practice various conventions of standard English.

Name _____

DIRECTIONS Use each word in a sentence.

income   expenses

_____

_____

_____

_____

DIRECTIONS Reread p. 32 of *Using Money*. In your own words, explain the difference between a need and a want. Use details from the text to support your answer.

_____

_____

_____

_____

Students show contextual understanding of Benchmark Vocabulary. Students write routinely for a range of tasks, purposes, and audiences.

DIRECTIONS Write an opinion paragraph supporting the point of view that creating and using a budget is an important practice. Be sure to include at least one reason and at least two facts and/or details that support each reason. Create a graphic organizer to show support for each reason. Then write your paragraph on the lines below.

_____
_____
_____
_____

Conventions

Relative Pronouns Underline the relative pronoun, and circle the word it modifies. Then write two of your own sentences that use relative pronouns.

1. Write down everything that you spend money on for one month.

2. People save for a vacation, which could cost a lot.

3. _____
_____

4. _____
_____

Students write routinely for a range of tasks, purposes, and audiences. Students practice various conventions of standard English.

Words from French

Word Bank

blond	encore	cuisine	critique
faux	genre	petite	chic
souvenir	soirée	sauté	brunette

Word Histories Write a list word for each description. Use a dictionary or thesaurus to help you.

1. light or yellowish hair   1. _____

2. something to remember a trip by   2. _____

3. dark or brownish hair.   3. _____

4. popular, stylish   4. _____

5. to offer detailed analysis   5. _____

6. small body frame, tiny   6. _____

7. the category of a text or composition   7. _____

8. fake, something that is not authentic   8. _____

9. additional performance at the end of a concert   9. _____

10. a party that takes place in the evening   10. _____

11. a style of cooking from a particular place   11. _____

12. to fry quickly in fat, a way to cook   12. _____

Students apply grade-level phonics and word analysis skills.

Name _____

DIRECTIONS Use each word in a sentence.

purchases   oversees

_____

_____

_____

_____

> **Write in Response to Reading**

DIRECTIONS Reread pp. 36–37 of *Using Money*. Write a paragraph explaining your opinion about whether people should be given another chance if they have been through a foreclosure. Use reasons and evidence from the text to support your answer.

_____

_____

_____

_____

_____

_____

Students show contextual understanding of Benchmark Vocabulary. Students write routinely for a range of tasks, purposes, and audiences.

Name _____

DIRECTIONS Write a short opinion essay about whether or not banks should be allowed to offer subprime mortgages. Your essay should state a clear opinion and provide at least two reasons supported by facts and details from the text. Remember to group related information. On a separate sheet of paper, create an outline or a graphic organizer to help you.

_____

_____

_____

_____

_____

_____

_____

Compound Sentences Use a comma and coordinating conjunction to rewrite the sentence below as a single compound sentence. Then write your own compound sentence that uses a comma and coordinating conjunction.

1. They get a loan from the bank. They promise to pay it back in a certain amount of time.

   _____

   _____

2. _____

   _____

Name _____

DIRECTIONS Use each word in a sentence.

organizations   research   scholarships

_____

_____

_____

_____

Write in Response to Reading

DIRECTIONS Reread pp. 38–41 of *Using Money*. Write a paragraph that explains how Warren Buffet makes money. Use reasons and evidence from the text to support your answer.

_____

_____

_____

_____

_____

_____

Students show contextual understanding of Benchmark Vocabulary. Students write routinely for a range of tasks, purposes, and audiences.

Name _____

DIRECTIONS Using evidence from the text, answer the following questions about pp. 38–41 of *Using Money*.

1. What is a coordinating conjunction?

   _____

   _____

2. Is it necessary that a writer use coordinating conjunctions?

   _____

   _____

   _____

3. Reread the second paragraph on p. 38. Identify one coordinating conjunction, and explain how it improves the text.

   _____

   _____

   _____

   _____

4. Reread pp. 40–41. Write a paragraph that explains what *shares* are. Use evidence from the text to support your answer.

   _____

   _____

   _____

   _____

Students analyze and respond to literary and informational text.

Name _____

DIRECTIONS Research a charity that you admire. Write a paragraph about why you are interested in this charity and why you might like to donate money to that organization. Remember to introduce your topic clearly, group related information into paragraphs, and quote accurately from sources.

_____

_____

_____

_____

_____

_____

_____

Conventions

Commas and Quotation Marks Use commas and quotation marks to correctly punctuate the sentence below. Then write three of your own sentences that include direct quotations from pp. 38–41 of *Using Money*.

1. In *Using Money*, Gail Fay writes Some investments, such as gold, are considered safe because the price is more likely to go up.

2. _____

_____

3. _____

_____

4. _____

_____

Students write routinely for a range of tasks, purposes, and audiences. Students practice various conventions of standard English.

Name _____

DIRECTIONS Use the word below in a sentence.

resemble

_____

_____

DIRECTIONS Reread pp. 42–43 of *Using Money*. Which do you think is a better place to save money—a piggy bank or an account with compound interest? Use evidence from the text to support your answer.

_____

_____

_____

_____

_____

_____

Students show contextual understanding of Benchmark Vocabulary. Students write routinely for a range of tasks, purposes, and audiences.

Name _____

DIRECTIONS Write an opinion paragraph about why you think it is important for a person to start saving money at a young age. You should support your opinion with reasons and evidence from the text. Conclude your paragraph with a strong statement that demonstrates the strength of your opinion.

_____

_____

_____

_____

_____

_____

_____

Conventions

Prepositional Phrases Underline the prepositional phrase in the sentence below. Then write three of your own sentences using prepositional phrases.

1. In some European countries today, people give piggy banks as gifts because they believe the pig brings good luck.

2. _____

   _____

3. _____

   _____

4. _____

   _____

Students write routinely for a range of tasks, purposes, and audiences. Students practice various conventions of standard English.

Name _____

DIRECTIONS Use each word in a sentence.

sternly   scornful   rotten

_____

_____

_____

_____

_____

Write in Response to Reading

DIRECTIONS Reread p. 8 of *A Tale of Two Poggles*. Why do you think Gloria Grabber hates the Internet? Use details and evidence from the text to support your answer.

_____

_____

_____

_____

_____

Students show contextual understanding of Benchmark Vocabulary. Students write routinely for a range of tasks, purposes, and audiences.

DIRECTIONS Using evidence from the text, answer the following questions about pp. 4–14 of *A Tale of Two Poggles*.

1. Reread pp. 6–7. What are some of Gloria Grabber's traits?

   _____

   _____

2. Reread pp. 10–11. What do Alejandro and Nina want to be when they get older?

   _____

   _____

3. Reread pp. 12–14. What did Alejandro and Nina write their stories about?

   _____

   _____

4. Why do you think Alejandro and Nina were selected as the winners?

   _____

   _____

   _____

5. Write a few sentences about what you think will happen when Alejandro and Nina visit the envelope factory.

   _____

   _____

   _____

   _____

Students analyze and respond to literary and informational text.

Name _____

DIRECTIONS Write an opinion paragraph about whether you think
it is better to write letters and put them in the mail, or to send e-mails
and text messages. Think about the way the townspeople, as well as
Gloria Grabber, feel about letters, envelopes, cell phones, e-mails, and
the Internet. Why do you think they have these feelings? Provide at least
three reasons that support your opinion. Use linking words and phrases to
connect your reasons.

_____

_____

_____

_____

_____

_____

_____

Conventions

Use Modal Auxiliaries Underline the modal auxiliary in the sentence.
Then write three of your own sentences using modal auxiliaries.

1. When people invest their money, they might use it in a way that will
   make more money in the future.

2. _____

   _____

3. _____

   _____

4. _____

   _____

Students write routinely for a range of tasks,
purposes, and audiences. Students practice
various conventions of standard English.

Name _____

DIRECTIONS Use each word in a sentence.

grimmer   miserable   automatically

_____

_____

_____

_____

Write in
Response to
Reading

DIRECTIONS Reread pp. 16–17 of *A Tale of Two Poggles*. What does the author's description of the envelope factory tell you about the townspeople's lives? Use specific details and evidence from the text to support your answer.

_____

_____

_____

_____

Students show contextual understanding of Benchmark Vocabulary. Students write routinely for a range of tasks, purposes, and audiences.

Writing

Name _____

DIRECTIONS Review the opinion you wrote in the previous lesson. Organize your ideas about the possible advantages and disadvantages for writing and sending letters versus sending emails and text messages. Select the strongest supporting examples. Then develop organized paragraphs that group related information about these advantages and disadvantages to support your opinion.

_____

_____

_____

_____

_____

_____

Conventions

Spell Correctly Cross out the misspelled words and write them on the line. Then write two of your own sentences, verifying the spelling of each word.

1. Hear are a few companies that are populer with investors.

_____

2. _____

_____

3. _____

_____

 Students write routinely for a range of tasks, purposes, and audiences. Students practice various conventions of standard English.

Name _____

Related Words

Word Bank

music	musician	select	selection
signal	part	impartial	electrician
protect	protection	magician	proper
properly	magic	electric	sign

DIRECTIONS   Write the list word that best completes each sentence below.

1. The store has a huge _____ of items.   1. _____

2. We called an _____ to fix the fuse box.   2. _____

3. I love listening to _____ on long car rides.   3. _____

4. It's important to do this job _____.   4. _____

5. This is my favorite _____ of the book.   5. _____

6. I learned a few _____ tricks on vacation!   6. _____

7. Mom said the _____ bill was due today.   7. _____

8. It's important that a judge remain _____.   8. _____

9. The _____ pulled a rabbit of her hat!   9. _____

10. A _____ is a person skilled in music.   10. _____

11. My mom showed me the _____ way to
    change a tire.   11. _____

12. The stop _____ on my street fell over.   12. _____

13. Please _____ one of the options below.   13. _____

14. Sometimes my cell phone _____ is very weak.   14. _____

15. The point of the game is to _____ the goalie. 15. _____

16. Police departments offer _____.   16. _____

Students apply grade-level phonics and word analysis skills.

Name _____

DIRECTIONS Use each word in a sentence.

revolve   enormous   distinctive

_____

_____

_____

_____

DIRECTIONS Reread pp. 23–32 of *A Tale of Two Poggles*. What is the theme of this story? Do you think there is more than one theme? Use details and evidence from the text to support your answer.

_____

_____

_____

_____

Students show contextual understanding of Benchmark Vocabulary. Students write routinely for a range of tasks, purposes, and audiences.

Name _____

DIRECTIONS Review the opinion piece that you have been working on. Research facts and information from reliable sources to support your opinions, reasons, and the advantages and disadvantages you have cited. If you encounter evidence that supports an opposing point of view, then take the time to listen to that argument and decide whether or not to accept it. Organize your research notes on the lines below.

_____

_____

_____

_____

_____

_____

Conventions

Progressive Verb Tenses Rewrite the sentence below using a progressive verb. Then write two of your own sentences about the town of Nether Poggle using progressive verb tenses.

1. Alejandro longed to become a pilot or conductor.

_____

_____

2. _____

_____

3. _____

_____

Students write routinely for a range of tasks, purposes, and audiences. Students practice various conventions of standard English.

Name _____

DIRECTIONS Use each word in a sentence.

cautiously   persuade   operate

_____

_____

_____

_____

_____

DIRECTIONS Reread pp. 38–39 of *A Tale of Two Poggles*. What is the significance of the word *money* as it is used in this text? Do you think Nina used the word on purpose to get Gloria's attention? Use details and evidence from the text to support your answer.

_____

_____

_____

_____

Students show contextual understanding of Benchmark Vocabulary. Students write routinely for a range of tasks, purposes, and audiences.

Name _____

DIRECTIONS Using evidence from the text, answer the following questions about pp. 33–40 of *A Tale of Two Poggles*.

1. Reread the dialogue on pp. 33–34. What do you learn about how the characters are feeling?

   _____

   _____

2. What words do you think are most responsible for creating the mood of their conversation?

   _____

   _____

3. Reread the dialogue on pp. 36–37. Why do you think the workers like the idea of turning the envelope factory into an amusement park?

   _____

   _____

4. Reread the first paragraph on p. 37. How does the author use punctuation to change the mood of the text?

   _____

   _____

Students analyze and respond to literary and informational text.

Writing

Name _____

DIRECTIONS Draft a paragraph about the method of communication you think is most effective—sending letters or writing emails. Provide detailed reasons that are supported by evidence. Remember to draw your evidence from the various sources you researched in the previous lesson.

_____

_____

_____

_____

_____

_____

_____

Conventions

Use Modal Auxiliaries Complete the partner activity on the lines below.

1. _____

   _____

2. _____

   _____

3. _____

   _____

4. _____

   _____

Students write routinely for a range of tasks, purposes, and audiences. Students practice various conventions of standard English.

Name _____

DIRECTIONS Use each word in a sentence.

transform local clever

_____

_____

_____

_____

DIRECTIONS Reread pp. 41–48 of *A Tale of Two Poggles*. Write a summary about the envelope factory's transformation into an amusement park. Use specific details from the text to support your answer.

_____

_____

_____

_____

_____

_____

Students show contextual understanding of Benchmark Vocabulary. Students write routinely for a range of tasks, purposes, and audiences.

Playing Sports and Giving Back

Professional sports teams make their fans cheer by winning games and championships. Winning is not just about scoring touchdowns, making baskets, and hitting homeruns, though. Many teams and players are winners because they help their communities. They know they are in a unique position to make a difference. Most are very happy to lend their names, time, autographed items, and money to help raise funds and awareness about important causes.

Some sports organizations choose certain charities to support. For example, Major League Baseball™ has chosen Boys & Girls Clubs of America™ as its official charity. Together, these two organizations help children learn to deal with barriers and challenges in their lives. Boys and girls are also taught about sportsmanship, responsibility, and team spirit.

The National Hockey League™ focuses its charity work on fighting cancer. In 1998, the league, along with the National Hockey League Players' Association™ started a program called Hockey Fights Cancer™. In 1999, the two organizations started the Hockey's All-Star Kids Foundation™. This program connects the hockey community with young people who have cancer and other serious diseases.

There are some causes many sports teams help support. One such cause is childhood obesity. When a child is obese, he or she weighs more than is healthy. This can lead to serious problems later in life. Today, more and more children are obese. Sports teams want to help children learn to take better care of their bodies. The Chicago Fire™, Denver Nuggets™, and Atlanta Falcons™ are just a few of the teams that help support programs to teach children about good nutrition and the importance of regular exercise. The National Football League™ started NFL PLAY 60™. This program encourages young football fans to be active for at least 60 minutes every day.

The Sports Philanthropy Project is an organization that helps sports teams give back to communities. It also keeps track of what teams and players are doing to make a difference. Do you want to know what your favorite teams and players are doing? Visit their Web sites to find out.

Students read text closely to determine what the text says.

Name _____

Gather Evidence How do professional athletes and teams lend their support? Underline two ways that are mentioned in the text.

Gather Evidence: Extend Your Ideas What specific causes do sports teams and players support?

_____

_____

Ask Questions Write three questions you might ask an athlete about giving back to his or her community.

_____

_____

Ask Questions: Extend Your Ideas Why do you think it is important for professional sports organizations to participate in charitable causes?

_____

_____

Make Your Case Circle the ways that sports teams help communities.

Make Your Case: Extend Your Ideas Using information from the text, explain what you think is the most important way that teams help communities.

_____

_____

Students read text closely to determine what the text says.

Name _____

DIRECTIONS Review the paragraph that you wrote in the previous lesson. Write a conclusion statement that sums up your opinion about the method of communication you think is better. End your paragraph by summarizing or restating your opinion. Then review your conclusion to ensure that you have added all of the necessary facts and details, and to delete any unnecessary or repeated information.

_____

_____

_____

_____

_____

_____

Conventions

Order Adjectives Write three descriptive sentences about Nether Poggle's new amusement park. Remember to order your adjectives correctly. Use details from pp. 41–48 of *A Tale of Two Poggles* to help you.

1. _____

_____

2. _____

_____

3. _____

_____

Students write routinely for a range of tasks, purposes, and audiences. Students practice various conventions of standard English.

Name _____

DIRECTIONS Use each word in a sentence.

captivated   inventions   appealing

_____

_____

_____

_____

_____

Write in Response to Reading

DIRECTIONS Reread pp. 94–107 of *The Boy Who Invented TV*. Do you think Philo would be an interesting person to have as a friend? Explain why or why not. Use details and examples from the text to support your answer.

_____

_____

_____

_____

_____

_____

_____

Students show contextual understanding of Benchmark Vocabulary. Students write routinely for a range of tasks, purposes, and audiences.

Name _____

DIRECTIONS Revisit *A Tale of Two Poggles* and *The Boy Who Invented TV*. Think about how each text discusses the way innovation leads to the creation of new products and services. Gather several examples from each text to support your opinion. Then draft an opening statement for a paragraph about which text you think does a better job of showing how innovation leads to new products and services.

_____

_____

_____

_____

_____

_____

Conventions

Order Adjectives Write three of your own sentences using multiple adjectives. Remember to order adjectives correctly.

1. _____

_____

2. _____

_____

3. _____

_____

Students write routinely for a range of tasks, purposes, and audiences. Students practice various conventions of standard English.

Name _____

DIRECTIONS Use each word in a sentence.

transmitting   devoured   revolutionary

_____

_____

_____

_____

_____

Write in Response to Reading

DIRECTIONS Reread pp. 108–120 of *The Boy Who Invented TV*. Based on the descriptive details in this section, explain why Philo keeps working toward his goal despite his many setbacks. Use details from the text to support your answer.

_____

_____

_____

_____

_____

Students show contextual understanding of Benchmark Vocabulary. Students write routinely for a range of tasks, purposes, and audiences.

Name _____

DIRECTIONS Using evidence from the text, answer the following questions about pp. 108–120 of *The Boy Who Invented TV.*

1. Explain Philo's phrase "capturing light in a bottle" as it relates to his idea to create television.

   _____

   _____

   _____

2. On p. 116, Philo tells Pem after they were married, "I have to tell you, there is another woman in my life—and her name is Television." What is Philo trying to tell Pem?

   _____

   _____

   _____

3. When Pem and their friends read the newspaper article they were "bouncing up and down." What does this descriptive detail tell you about this event?

   _____

   _____

   _____

4. On p. 120 the author calls Philo "a shaper of the world to come." What does this descriptive detail help you understand?

   _____

   _____

   _____

Students analyze and respond to literary and informational text.

Name _____

DIRECTIONS Plan and prewrite for an opinion essay in which you state and support your opinion about whether you believe innovation is needed for economic growth. Create an organizational T-chart with your opinion at the top. List your reasons for having that opinion on the left. Then plan your opinion writing by gathering evidence from *Using Money, A Tale of Two Poggles,* and *The Boy Who Invented TV*. Record any evidence that you gather on the right side of the T-chart.

Conventions

Mark Direct Speech and Quotations Select two different pieces of text from *The Boy Who Invented TV*. Write those quotations on the lines below. Remember to use quotation marks and commas correctly.

1. _____

_____

2. _____

_____

Students write routinely for a range of tasks, purposes, and audiences. Students practice various conventions of standard English.

Name _____

Greek Roots

Word Bank

geology	microcosm	microbe	automation	graphics
autonomous	photographer	autodidact	biosphere	terminology
zoology	paleontology	epigraph	photosynthesis	biographer

DIRECTIONS   Write the list word that best fits each group.

1. animal, study, science, _____   1. _____

2. Earth, rocks, mountains, _____   2. _____

3. bacteria, tiny, organism, _____   3. _____

4. specific terms, theory, profession, _____   4. _____

5. researcher, writer, _____   5. _____

6. professional, camera, _____   6. _____

7. fossils, science, digging, _____   7. _____

8. factory, assembly line, _____   8. _____

9. picture, facts, images, _____   9. _____

Definitions   Write the list word that fits the definition. Use a dictionary or thesaurus to help you.

10. a person who is self-taught   10. _____

11. the way plants get food from sunlight   11. _____

12. having self-government, or power   12. _____

13. an inscription on a building or statue   13. _____

14. a community or place used as an example   14. _____

15. regions of the Earth occupied by living creatures   15. _____

Students apply grade-level phonics and word analysis skills.

Name _____

DIRECTIONS Use each word in a sentence.

service   charges   captivated   inventions

_____

_____

_____

_____

_____

_____

**Write in
Response to
Reading**

DIRECTIONS Revisit *Using Money* and *The Boy Who Invented TV*. How can readers determine which information is important in a text, and which is not? Use examples from both texts to support your answer.

_____

_____

_____

_____

_____

Students show contextual understanding
of Benchmark Vocabulary. Students write
routinely for a range of tasks, purposes, and
audiences.

Name _____

DIRECTIONS Write an opinion essay about whether or not you believe innovation is needed for economic growth. Review your chart from the previous lesson, and make a final decision about whether you have chosen the best details to support your opinion. Remember to use linking words to connect details from the text with your own opinions.

_____

_____

_____

_____

_____

_____

_____

_____

_____

Conventions

Relative Pronouns Circle the relative pronoun. Underline the noun it modifies. Then write your own sentence using relative pronouns.

1. Charities are organizations that accept money gifts to provide help to people in need.

2. Philo was a real inventor, someone who helped shape the future.

3. The stock market is not like a food market, which has a physical location.

4. _____

_____

Students write routinely for a range of tasks, purposes, and audiences. Students practice various conventions of standard English.

Name _____

Greek & Latin Suffixes

Word Bank

compartment	revolutionize	amendment	emphasize	triviality
summarize	contentment	judgment	fantasize	conceptualize
celebrity	poverty	idolize	enmity	allotment

DIRECTIONS Write the list word that fits the definition. Use a dictionary or thesaurus to help you.

1. an amount of something meant for someone in particular

1. _____

2. a separate section, often for storage

2. _____

3. a statement about the main points of something

3. _____

4. being hostile toward something

4. _____

5. to daydream, or imagine something

5. _____

6. a state of deep satisfaction

6. _____

7. to change something radically

7. _____

8. of little value, not important

8. _____

9. to give special attention to

9. _____

10. the ability to make decisions or draw conclusions

10. _____

11. to imagine, or envision something

11. _____

12. to admire someone or something intensely

12. _____

13. a famous person

13. _____

14. a change to a document

14. _____

15. the state of being very poor

15. _____

Students apply grade-level phonics and word analysis skills.

Name _____

DIRECTIONS Use each word in a sentence.

intelligence   vacuum   alien

_____

_____

_____

_____

Write in Response to Reading

DIRECTIONS Reread Scene 1 of *RoBo Cleaner*. Do you think it's possible to determine a drama's theme from the first scene only? Use details from the text to support your answer.

_____

_____

_____

_____

_____

Students show contextual understanding of Benchmark Vocabulary. Students write routinely for a range of tasks, purposes, and audiences.

DIRECTIONS Using evidence from the text, answer the following questions about *RoBo Cleaner*.

1. What do you think is the main theme of *RoBo Cleaner*?

_____

_____

2. List four details from the text that directly support this theme.

Detail 1: _____

_____

Detail 2: _____

_____

Detail 3: _____

_____

Detail 4: _____

_____

3. Reread Scene 7. Write about a time that you had trouble using a new technology. Was it similar to the events in Scene 7? Tell what happened and explain why or why not. Use evidence from the text to support your answer.

_____

_____

_____

_____

_____

Students analyze and respond to literary and informational text.

Name _____

DIRECTIONS Revise, edit, and proofread the opinion essay you have been working on. Write your essay on the lines below.

_____

_____

_____

_____

_____

_____

_____

_____

_____

_____

Conventions

Compound Sentences Write three of your own compound sentences.

1. _____

_____

2. _____

_____

3. _____

_____

Students write routinely for a range of tasks, purposes, and audiences. Students practice various conventions of standard English.

Name _____

DIRECTIONS Use each word in a sentence.

expenses   automatically   appealing

_____

_____

_____

_____

Write in Response to Reading

DIRECTIONS Revisit *Using Money* and *The Boy Who Invented TV*. Do you think Philo was a saver or a spender? Use evidence from both texts to support your answer.

_____

_____

_____

_____

Students show contextual understanding of Benchmark Vocabulary. Students write routinely for a range of tasks, purposes, and audiences.

Name _____

DIRECTIONS Publish and present the opinion essays you have been working on. First, draft a plan for your presentation on the lines below. If you feel it is necessary, alter your writing. Then present your writing to the class.

_____

_____

_____

_____

_____

_____

Conventions

Prepositional Phrases Underline the prepositional phrases. Then write two of your own sentences that use prepositional phrases.

1. On clear summer nights, as they lay in the grass and gazed at the stars, his father told him about inventors.

2. Instead of handwriting a check, you electronically transfer money over the Internet from your account to the company you want to pay.

3. _____

_____

4. _____

_____

Students write routinely for a range of tasks, purposes, and audiences.
Students practice various conventions of standard English.